The
Complete
Guide *to*
Funeral
Planning

D0111468

The Complete Guide *to* Funeral Planning

How to Arrange the Appropriate Service

GEOFFREY C. CARNELL

THE LYONS PRESS
Guilford, Connecticut
An imprint of The Globe Pequot Press

The Lyons Press is an imprint of The Globe Pequot Press.

Canadian edition published in 1998 as *When the Sun Sets: A Guide to Funeral Planning* by Breakwater Books, P.O. Box 2188, 100 Water Street, St. John's, Newfoundland, Canada A1C 6E6.

Printed in the United States of America

10   9   8   7   6   5   4   3   2   1

Canadian design and production: Nadine Osmond

Editing: Canadian editor, rev. ed., Jocelyne Thomas
         American editor, Lisa Purcell

ISBN 1-59228-441-8

Library of Congress Cataloging-in-Publication Data is available on file.

Dedicated to the memory of my father
Geoffrey C. Carnell, Sr.
1915–1987

Table of Contents

Acknowledgments

Grateful acknowledgment is made to a family friend, Colin Jamieson, who approached me about writing an article on funeral planning for the first issue of his new Senior's Newspaper, *50 Plus: The New Age Senior.* It was due to his encouragement and vision that one simple article led to a series of articles from which this book was adapted.

I benefited greatly from information provided regularly by Batesville Canada about their innovative services, products, and merchandising techniques. And from all those writers, some of whom are mentioned herein, who have written and continue to write about similar topics.

I acknowledge with thanks the management, funeral directors, and office staff at Carnell's Funeral Home for their thoughtful comments, advice, and ideas relating to this book and the series of articles leading up to it.

In the United States, I wish to thank The Lyons Press for bringing this book to an American audience.

Finally, I wish to thank the Canadian Publisher, Clyde Rose, for believing in and guiding the project, and his dedicated, enthusiastic and professional staff at Breakwater Books, in particular, Marketing Coordinator,

Jennifer Holden; Executive Assistant, Michelle Cable-Foote; Production Coordinator, Carla Kean; Designer, Nadine Osmond; Marketing Assistant, Rebecca Rose, and last but by no means least, for revised editing, Jocelyne Thomas.

The Complete Guide *to* Funeral Planning

Chapter One
Why We Need
to Say Goodbye

Fare thee well! and if forever,
Still forever, fare thee well.
                    —Byron, *Fare thee Well*

I nvariably, the subject of funerals and their value receives less than favorable treatment from the media in particular and from people in general. Journalists tend to focus on the tangible costs of the funeral, rather than the intangible value of the services provided. This leads some people to conclude that the whole business of funeralization, as it is commonly known in the profession, has little worth beyond the final bill that must be paid. Yet, such a notion could not be more wrong. The significance of funeralization goes far beyond the profit it offers to those who provide the goods and services that constitute today's funeral.

In his award-winning essay, "None are Invited, But All May Come—The Value of Funeralization," Richard Rancourt, a graduate of the Funeral Services Education Program at Kingstec Community College in Kentville, Nova Scotia, Canada, summed up why people need funeral and memorial services. Interestingly, Rancourt found the inspiration for his ideas on a classroom bulletin board, so their true author remains unknown. According to Rancourt, funerals do some or all of the following:

- Confirm the reality and finality of death.
- Provide a climate for mourning and the expression of grief.
- Allow the sorrows of one to become the sorrows of many.
- Enable the community to pay respect.
- Encourage the affirmation of religious faith.
- Celebrate the life that has been lived.
- Spur people to give love without expecting something in return.

Confirming Death's Reality

Many authors who write about the subject believe that, as a society, we do not deal with death very well. In American culture, the most common responses to the subject of death are either avoidance or denial. Fear is at the heart of both reactions. It is human nature to fear the unknown, and there is nothing that is as foreign to us as death. In *The Gift of Significance*, Doug Manning writes, "A great deal of our reluctance to face death is the fear of intimacy." Indeed, there are few things that are as intimate as the thoughts and feelings surrounding the death of a loved one.

The very act of funeralization forces people to face the reality of death. The authors of *The Last Dance,* explain how this happens, "Making arrangements for the disposition of the body engages the survivor in a process that helps reinforce the recognition that the deceased is really dead." This is the process of closure.

The preparation of the deceased for viewing is another step to assist the bereaved in the grief process. Whether or not others view the remains is a matter of personal choice for a family, but it is often important for the family members themselves to view their deceased loved one. Although a painful occasion, it ultimately begins the healing process, as it allows the bereaved family a chance to mourn and express the grief that must be communicated.

Enabling the Community to Pay Respect

In times when we must carry heavy burdens, such as the death of a loved one, the heaviness of sorrow is often lightened by the notion that others around us must bear the same weight. It is as if caring for one another helps us lighten each other's loads. Funerals allow for this communal caring and sharing because they enable us to mourn together, thereby serving not only a psychological function, but a social one as well. Our presence in a time of need says, "I'll be there for you."

And when we care for one another at a time of death, we do things for people without expectation of return, such as sending flowers, making in memoriam donations, or bringing food to the grieving family. All of this is part of the total process of funeralization. A funeral allows people to pay their respects and share burdens. To ignore the gathering together for the ceremony of a funeral deprives us from saying, "I'll be there," to those who need to know someone cares.

Celebrating Faith and a Life Lived

For a majority of funerals, some sort of affirmation of religious faith is an integral part of the ceremony. It allows mourners to share deeply held beliefs by expressing them openly. The authors of *The Last Dance* assert that these "ceremonies give significance to the events that lead to the final disposition of the deceased's body."

A funeral is an opportunity to show the significance of a person in the lives of mourners and the community at large. This significance is not measured simply by the purchase of merchandise or the presence of hundreds of people. It is demonstrated by the very act of the funeral itself. Each family has its own way of recognizing the significance of a life that has been lived. They celebrate and remember the deceased by sharing stories and memories during the visitation period or by some symbolic gesture at the church or graveside.

When a funeral gives a family the opportunity to think about the life of the loved one who has died, then the funeral is healthy. When friends are there to share how important the deceased was to them, then the funeral is healthy. When the words expressed help the family to face a loss, then the funeral is healthy.

In *The Gift of Significance,* Doug Manning states: "If we lose the funeral, we will lose one of the most helpful steps in the healing process.... Stated briefly, significance means: no one is dead until they are forgotten." Therefore, we must not forget about the value of funerals and importance of funeral rituals.*

* The previous three sections were adapted from "None are Invited, But All May Come The Value of Funeralization," by Richard Rancourt. Used by kind permission of the Funeral Service Association of Canada.

The Value of Funeral Rituals

Every funeral is different. Many factors contribute to the individuality of a funeral, but none has a more profound effect than the use of rituals. Yet, what is a ritual and how does it relate to the loss of a loved one and the type of funeral service chosen? These questions can be answered with some simple examples.

We often read or hear about news events that result in a loss of life. Whether these deaths result from an explosion, plane crash, or shooting, in the days that follow these tragedies, a number of events underscore the human need for ritual. People place flowers at the site where the event occurred. Others wear black arm bands. Flags fly at half-staff. Memorial services are held or monuments are erected with the names of all those who died. These are the common rituals to observe death that offer many people a chance to share sympathy with those who have experienced the loss personally.

Rituals come in many different forms and are limited only by the boundaries of the imagination. Some rituals may be personal, while others may be communal and supportive. But all provide a sense of continuity and therapy for those mourning a loss. Because of their experience, funeral directors can be both providers and designers of rituals, but the best ideas come from loving, caring families, as the following example illustrates.

A common ritual performed by funeral directors at a graveside committal service is to sprinkle sand over the casket or urn when the clergy says, "earth to earth, ashes to ashes, dust to dust." In most cases, the funeral director uses a small brass holder, called a "shaker," containing silica sand. On one occasion, just before the start of a funeral service, a funeral director was approached by the deceased man's son, who carried a small bottle of sand. The sand had come from his father's birthplace, and he asked that it be used instead of the traditional shaker. The funeral director suggested that the son perform the ritual of sprinkling the special sand over his father's casket. At the end of the service, after emptying the majority of the sand into the grave, the son kept a small portion as a symbol of the cherished memories of his father. This ritual meant a great deal to the son, but it also deeply moved those who attended the committal service. We learn rituals from others, and we share them as well.

There are many rituals, all holding special meaning for those who mourn. Rituals also symbolize what was unique about the deceased, such as his or her profession or interest.

At a service for a firefighter, his casket was carried from the church to the cemetery by a fire truck. In another case, a harness racer's favorite horse and buggy led the funeral procession to his graveside.

When a loved one dies, rituals fill a need, not only for the members of the family, but for the community as well. They offer comfort and strengthen us spiritually, psychologically, and socially. Most religions, for example, observe a number of rituals during a time of death, such as the use of a pall, holy water, or incense. Selected scripture readings, hymns, and prayers are other rituals that add special meaning to a service.

In the Jewish faith, it is customary at the cemetary for the men to walk the casket to the graveside. Once lowered to the bottom of the grave, shovels of earth are then placed over the casket by some of those in attendance.

Psychologically, mourners are comforted by such rituals as writing a last letter to the deceased, placing mementos in the casket, or completing memorial parchments. As a group, we take comfort by visiting the funeral home, giving "in memoriam" gifts, sending flowers, or attending the funeral service, all of which demonstrate our sharing of sympathy.

Even those rituals to prepare and view a loved one's remains have value. From the preparations of the body to the selection of clothing and personal effects, these time-honored rituals ensure that the loved one is treated with care and dignity. And finally, the act of the funeral service respects and strengthens the cultural rituals dictated by a family's nationality, religious affiliation, or beliefs. Every funeral service should respect the rituals and customs of those involved. Such rituals are the cornerstone of a funeral service and are essential to those who mourn. Their value cannot be underestimated.

Chapter Two
How to Help

Though they go mad they shall be sane,
Though they sink through the sea they shall rise again;
Though lovers be lost love shall not;
And death shall have no dominion.
                    —Dylan Thomas, *25 Poems*

For many people, a funeral home can be a very intimidating place, particularly for those who have never been in one before or have not experienced the death of a family member or close friend. And even those who have suffered a loss may still feel awkward about coming to a funeral home or facing the mourning family.

How often have you thought, "I don't know what to say," or "What can I do to help?" as you considered going to a funeral home or you heard about the death of a relative, friend, or neighbor? This is quite natural, but there are simple actions that show support and offer comfort to both the bereaved and ourselves.

There is nothing more comforting to a bereaved family than simply being there for them. You can do this by attending the funeral service, visiting the family home, coming to the funeral home, telephoning, or sending a letter or card of condolence. By being there, whether in person or in spirit, you show the family that their friends care about them very much.

This gesture should not end when the funeral ends. Often, it is just as important to be there after the funeral. The days and weeks that follow can be the most difficult for the survivors. Their feelings of loneliness, confusion, and fear can be quite overwhelming, but can be alleviated by a phone call, letter, or visit.

What to Say

Everyone expresses feelings differently, but when someone has died, even the most eloquent person can be lost for words or unsure of what to say. Try to avoid clichés such as:

- You're doing so well.
- I know just how you feel.
- You'll be all right.
- Time will take care of everything.

Although well-intentioned, the bereaved family may feel misunderstood or upset over such presumptions. Instead of suggesting how they should or will feel, let them tell you the emotions they are experiencing and help them express them. Try such phrases as:

- How are you feeling?
- This must be very hard for you.
- How is everyone coping?

Sometimes nothing needs to be said. A warm embrace or handshake is all that is necessary to show how much you care, particularly if there is a large crowd at the funeral home and conversation is restricted.

Show Your Feelings

It's okay to cry. It is a way to acknowledge your loss. Tears are not a sign of weakness. It is fine to cry with the bereaved family. It is a positive outlet for your emotions and actually makes you and family members feel better.

It's okay to laugh, too. On many occasions, it is not uncommon to hear loud laughter coming from a funeral home visitation room or lounge. At these times, family and friends are recounting humorous incidents they heard about or have had with the deceased. Laughter is another positive emotion that helps the pain dissipate and the healing to begin. Do not be reluctant to share in or contribute to these moments of laughter and enjoyment. There is no ban on laughter when celebrating the life of a loved one.

Many gestures allow relatives and friends to express their feelings and support to a bereaved family. The death announcement in the newspaper can give real insight into some of the gestures that hold special meaning for the family. In these announcements, families may opt to say, "flowers gratefully accepted," or "in lieu of flowers, donations may be made (to a specific charity)," to give guidance to sympathetic well-wishers. Families make such comments about flowers and donations after careful consideration of the importance of certain causes or charities to the deceased. One may also purchase sympathy or mass cards and either bring them to the family during the funeral home visit or send them after the funeral service.

After the Funeral

Grief does not end with the funeral. Healing is a long process that may require months or even years. As a friend or family member to the bereaved, you can help by continuing to call and visit, dropping by with food, or offering to babysit or take the children for the day. Try to remember such special days as holidays, birthdays, and anniversaries, which can be especially difficult for the bereaved.

Recently, some funeral homes have begun to provide grief assistance or "aftercare" programs. In *The Complete Funeral Guide*, Patricia A. Simone defines "aftercare" as a service for assisting families through the practical issues after death as well as offering assistance through the grieving process.

Depending on the resources available, some funeral directors either provide some form of bereavement follow-up themselves or hire specialists in grief counselling and therapy to join their staff. Other funeral directors are reluctant to enter into bereavement support services themselves because of a lack of formal training, but are happy to refer families and friends to such programs in the community. Ultimately, during the execution of their normal duties, funeral directors can directly influence the grief of the survivors they serve and impact the resolution of that grief. Through their advice and counsel, funeral directors give early aid in the grief process and help survivors take their first steps to adjust to their loss and resume a meaningful life. Funeral directors often assist the bereaved by:

- Compiling and making available free information and resource materials.
- Distributing these materials to individuals and organizations associated with bereavement support.

- Establishing libraries with pamphlets, books, and audio-visual aids.
- Serving as a liaison between some of the support groups in the community.
- Establishing alliances with members of support groups.
- Designating a knowledgeable person on their staff for follow-up work and post-funeral visits.
- Developing community education programs through the sponsorship of seminars.
- Distributing Help Letters which are a professionally written monthly publication to families.

Barbara Hills Les Strang, founder and publisher of the Afterloss Grief Recovery Program put it best. She said: "Grief is a journey the heart makes alone. No one can recover from our grief for us and no one can recover from our grief but us. And grief doesn't just go away like some people say. What every bereaved person needs is simply a chance: a chance to learn what we can do to help ourselves so we can recover."

Chapter Three

The First Steps

*I can't think of a more wonderful thanksgiving
for the life I have had than that everyone
should be jolly at my funeral.*
—Lord Louis Mountbatten

What should a person do first upon learning of a loved one's death? When someone dies, there are certain procedures to follow before funeral preparations can be made. These will depend on a number of factors. For example, should death occur far from home, tasks to ensure safe passage of a loved one's remains to the place of burial or cremation will have to be done. The following are some of those first steps that must be taken upon the death of a loved one.

Death at Home

If a loved one dies in his or her own home or that of a family member, the following professionals should be contacted, depending on the circumstances surrounding the death:

- In all circumstances, a physician must be contacted. This physician must verify that death has occurred and must sign the death certificate.

- If a sudden, unexpected, or accidental death occurs, the police must be contacted. If an emergency 911 call is placed, the information received will automatically be conveyed to the police department. Police will respond along with the ambulance service.
- A funeral director can be contacted, as his or her presence can help to relieve the family of the problems and details surrounding a death at home.
- A member of the clergy, rabbi, or other spiritual leader can be contacted, depending upon the deceased's or family's beliefs or religious affiliations.

After death is pronounced, the police or physician will authorize the transfer of the remains either to the hospital for an autopsy or to the funeral home. In both cases, the funeral director can handle the transportation of the remains.

Legally, the services of a medical examiner or coroner are required under the following circumstances:

- When an individual has not been under the recent and regular care of a physician.
- When accidental death occurs.
- When death results from something other than natural causes.

If the medical examiner or coroner requests a postmortem examination, commonly called an autopsy, the family cannot object. If the attending or family physician requests an autopsy, the family's consent is required. Family members may also request that an autopsy be

---

performed should they wish to confirm the cause of death or obtain a greater understanding of their loved one's medical history.

Death at a Resident Care Facility

Many people who live in resident care facilities leave specific instructions with the administrator or superintendent as to whom should be contacted in the event of their death. These instructions should include the name of the funeral home of choice. The funeral director would then be contacted. If no autopsy is required, the remains would be transferred immediately to the funeral home since resident care facilities do not usually have morgues. Funeral arrangements can then be made by family members or the facility's staff, who follow those instructions left by the deceased.

Death in Hospital

The procedure followed when death occurs in a hospital is similar to that of a resident care facility. Transfer of the remains to the funeral home would be more flexible because hospitals do have morgues. The only delays that may be encountered with a hospital death would be the completion of an autopsy or the signing of the death certificate by the attending physician.

Once a death certificate is received by the funeral director, it is the responsibility of the funeral home to ensure that it is completed accurately and filed with the Registrar of the District in which the death occured. A copy is also forwarded to the State Registrar. Generally, funeral homes do not release copies of the original death certificate, but certified copies are available to family members from the District or State Registrar.

Death while Traveling

If a loved one dies while he or she is traveling, the family members may choose one of the following options:

- Contact a representative from a funeral home in the community in which the loved one normally lived. This is generally recommended because the funeral director will make the necessary arrangements to transport the remains back home. All funeral arrangements can then be made, face-to-face, between family members and this local funeral home.
- Contact a representative from a funeral home in the location where death occurred. Transportation arrangements would then be made by this funeral home to ensure the remains were transferred to a funeral home in the community where the deceased lived or where family members reside.
- If immediate cremation is the family's wish, a funeral home in the place of death can be contacted. The loved one could be cremated in the community where he or she died, with the cremated remains interred or scattered by the family later.

Donating to Medical Science

When one dies and has specified that the body be donated to medical science, all rights to the body including its final disposition are assigned to the medical school. Most medical schools will pay for the nearby transportation, preparation, and final disposition of the deceased. Some, however, do not provide funds for the initial preparation and transportation, but will pay all other expenses including cremation and conveyance of the cremated remains to a place specified by the donor or their family.

A medical school will generally release the body or cremated remains to the family for burial anywhere from 6 months to 36 months after the date of death. Usually the body is cremated, with burial or scattering in a university plot. In fact, some universities have their own crematories. If a place of final disposition cannot be provided by the donor's family, the cremated remains will be stored by the medical school for a specified period, after which they are disposed of in a dignified and respectful manner.

Because of the importance of the early preservation of the body, a memorial service is often held shortly after the donor's death. This is usually followed by a short committal service at graveside at the time the remains are returned to the family or designated funeral home.

If cremation is not desired, the donor's family can make arrangements with a funeral home to bury or entomb the remains in accordance with their wishes.

There is no guarantee a donor's body will be accepted. Some medical schools may not have an immediate need or provision for storage. Furthermore, the cause of death and condition of the body may render it inappropriate for medical education. A few schools take care of the final disposition of the donor's remains regardless of condition at the time of death, in order to fulfill their contract with the donor. Alternate arrangements, however, should be made with a funeral home in the event the donor's body is not accepted.

Transporting a Loved One Back Home

If a person dies while traveling or living in another state or country, and the family decides to transport the remains home for burial or cremation, some preparation will be necessary to meet requirements on airlines or other modes of transportation.

The family may choose to either work with their local funeral home or with one in the community where the loved one died. If death occurred in a community that is not well-known to the surviving family members, working with their own local funeral home is recommended.

For shipping a loved one's remains within the U.S., some preparation and embalming is necessary to meet the carrier's requirements. The carrier will accept a casket or a shipping container specially designed for this purpose. If the remains are shipped in a casket, it must be enclosed in a wooden case with handles or in a shipping tray consisting of a rigid tray with sidewalls and a protective cover. If a shipping container is used, the remains will be removed at the receiving funeral home and placed in a casket.

As it is traditional in the Jewish faith not to embalm or view the deceased, the remains are wrapped in a special burial shroud. To meet carrier requirements the shrouded body is placed in a shipping container and packed with dry ice to prevent decomposition and odor.

The deceased must be shipped in an airtight steel casket or in a wooden casket with a steel inner liner under any of the following circumstances:

- When death resulted from an infectious or contagious disease.

- When death occurred some time earlier.
- When the remains have been disinterred, or removed from a previous grave or tomb.

All shipments must be accompanied by the proper documents, which are placed in a specially designed envelope attached to the outside container. All documents can be prepared or procured by the funeral director. Necessary documents include:

- Certified death certificate
- True copy of death certificate
- Embalmer's report
- Embassy travel affidavits
- Burial permit
- Letter from medical examiner authorizing transportation and verifying that there were no communicable diseases
- Declaration of contents, issued by funeral home
- Other documents required by various jurisdictions involved, including foreign countries

Airlines will also accept and ship cremated remains suitably packaged, labeled, and accompanied by all applicable documents, as noted above. If the cremated remains are to be conveyed by a family member, they may be carried as hand luggage or checked in. In addition to the details mentioned above, the shipping funeral director will arrange all flights and confirm them with the director of the receiving funeral home or designated consignee.

The shipment of remains to a foreign country is not unlike shipments within the U.S. Each country, however, has specific rules and regulations that must be strictly followed. Failure to comply with the regulations of the country of destination may result in refusal to permit entry of the shipment and subsequent return to the shipping funeral home. Funeral directors will be aware of these foreign regulations, or will know where to find the answers.

Shipping Services

Regardless of the country where the death occurred, your local funeral director would be familiar with or could readily access the rules and regulations associated with the transportation of the deceased. Many funeral homes that are contacted by families outside their regular service area engage specialty firms to provide shipping assistance services. These firms have established worldwide shipping networks. Once contacted by your local funeral home and given the pertinent information about the deceased, they will contact a service representative in the area where the death occurred. The service representative will look after all repatriation details, including information concerning the release and condition of the remains, flight scheduling, and documentation.

In recent years, airlines have expanded and enhanced their services for the transfer of human remains. For example, by switching from weight-based rates to flat rates based on destination, the airlines have made it easier for funeral directors to quote shipment rates to families. Airlines also book passage on flights for those who are escorting human remains and guarantee that escorts will not be bumped from a flight if it is oversold. They will also make sure escorts are given special treatment at the boarding gate, during the flight, and at the destination. Airlines also offer "compassionate travel fares" to anyone who must travel due to the death of an immediate family member. If eligible, a partial refund of the fare is available to travelers making a round trip.

If a traveler had purchased cancellation or travel insurance before dying, this insurance may cover some or all of the expenses related to a funeral director's repatriation services. Depending on the insurance company, the policy could contain a cash benefit, excluding the cost of the casket, to cover all or a portion of the homeward transportation of the deceased, insured person to the original place of departure by the most direct route.

In addition to the benefits payable with cancellation insurance, refunds may also be due from unused travel expenses. As all policies are different, it is always wise before traveling to review the policy documents and/or ask your booking agent to provide a summary of the coverage and benefits available under the policy.

The Death Certificate

The first and most important document to be completed when a death occurs is the death certificate. Without it, final care and disposition of the deceased cannot take place. In addition to its importance in the burial and repatriation of the deceased, the registered copy of the death certificate or a similar document verifying proof of death is required by many insurance companies, financial institutions, and government agencies in matters pertaining to the settlement of the deceased's estate.

To be valid, a death certificate must be signed by the attending physician or family physician who is familiar with the deceased's medical history. Most hospitals will not release a loved one's remains until the certificate is signed. This can cause delays for the funeral home to receive the remains, particularly on weekends and holidays when the physician is not working. This, in turn, delays the preparation of the remains for viewing.

To accurately complete the medical information required on the certificate, the physician may require an autopsy to verify or determine the cause of death. If the death is sudden, unexpected, or a result of foul play, and the medical examiner or coroner calls for an autopsy, the family cannot overrule this decision. Yet, even if death was natural, a family may choose to have an autopsy performed to verify the specific cause or to seek more information about the deceased's medical history that may assist his or her children or grandchildren.

Once the loved one's body is ready for release from a hospital, the funeral director conducting the removal will be given the original death certificate, which is still incomplete at this point. It becomes the funeral home's responsibility to complete and register it. Completing the death certificate usually involves verifying personal information about the deceased such as age, date of birth, principal residence, employer, burial information, and family details, like the names and birthplaces of the deceased's mother and father. Shortly after the funeral service, the original death certificate is registered with the Registrar of the District in which the death occurred and a copy forwarded to the State Registrar.

If an expected death occurs at home, the funeral director may bring a blank death certificate to the home for the family physician to complete during the removal of the remains to the funeral home. If not in attendance, the physician may give a verbal approval over the telephone to the funeral director and family to remove the remains. Shortly thereafter, the funeral director would go to the physician's office or home to get the certificate signed.

Regardless of one's citizenship, when an individual dies outside his or her own country, the death must be registered in the country in which the death occurred. In a case where death occurs in international waters, death must be registered in the country to which the remains are conveyed. In these cases, the death certificate becomes a critical document in the repatriation process. Since the original certificate must be registered, embassies will require both a registered copy, which does not contain the cause of death, and a notarized copy, which has been verified as a true copy by a notary or commissioner of oaths.

These, along with other documents, are placed in an envelope attached to the shipping container for inspection by customs officials. Errors in the preparation of these documents can cause undue delay and hardship for families awaiting the return of their loved one.

In theory, the registration of the death certificate should take place before the burial of the deceased. Once registered, an Application and Permit For Disposition of Human Remains is completed by the funeral director or person in charge of the disposition. The Permit accompanies the remains to the place of disposition and is then forwarded by the funeral director or person in charge of the disposition to the Registrar of the District in which disposition occured. In the case when the remains are cremated and scattered at sea, the Permit must be forwarded to the District nearest the point where the cremated remains were scattered.

Chapter Four

The First Call

When I can read my title clear
To mansions in the skies,
I'll bid farewell to every fear,
And wipe my weeping eyes.
                    — Isaac Watts, *Hymns & Spiritual Songs*

The title of funeral director is a relatively new one. For years, individuals who looked after a loved one when death occurred were commonly referred to as "undertakers" or "morticians." The origins of these former titles were linked to some facet of the business or service provided. For example, undertakers were those persons in a community who would undertake to care for and prepare the deceased for burial. The title for morticians was derived from their place of employment, which was known as a mortuary.

Regardless of the title used, the role of those individuals entrusted with the care and preparation of the dead for final disposition has changed significantly. Historically, family members, nurses, cemetery staff, livery men, carpenters, and others were involved. Today, other than in remote areas where a local priest, other spiritual leader, or public official could be granted authority, licensed funeral directors and embalmers perform or coordinate all of these functions.

Because of the different practices and customs followed by some religious faiths, funeral directors and embalmers are not always involved with the preparation of the deceased. For those faiths that do not permit embalming, the deceased is washed, wrapped in a shroud, and placed in a simple wooden casket by appointed specialists or members of that faith community. When a funeral home is available, this ritual is performed privately in a preparation room.

And although the number of funerals preplanned or prepaid is growing annually, the majority are usually arranged immediately after death. Therefore, the first call to the funeral home telling of a death and requesting the services of a funeral director is often very important. It is helpful to have some idea of what to expect from this first call.

The importance of the first call cannot be overemphasized. A funeral director requires certain basic information in order to effectively undertake his or her duties on behalf of the family. It is understandable that the person who calls may be a very upset and distraught family member who finds it difficult to respond effectively. In cases like these, the family member may wait to regain composure before calling or designate someone else to make the call. It is not uncommon for funeral directors to receive calls from hospital staff, physicians, members of the clergy, business associates, or friends of the deceased or family. As long as the caller has some knowledge about the deceased and the type of funeral services desired, anyone may call.

During this first call, the funeral director will request the following information:

- Full name of the deceased
- Place of death
- Name of person calling and relationship to deceased
- Home address of the deceased
- Family phone numbers
- Physician's name
- Whether or not an autopsy is required,
- Whether a funeral notice is to be prepared immediately and information pertinent to it
- Convenient time to meet with family or friends to discuss funeral arrangements

Embalming

If, for any reason, the funeral arrangement meeting must be delayed, the funeral director may also inquire as to the type of funeral service required and seek permission to commence embalming procedures.

Embalming is the art of disinfecting remains and thereby slowing the process of decomposition. The embalmer also does restorative work and applies cosmetics as necessary.* Legally, embalming is not generally required for disposition. It may be required, however, when sending remains out of the state or country, unless contrary to certain religious beliefs. It is also required by many common carriers prior to shipment.

If embalming was not required, the casket would remain closed during the visitation period or wake. If the

---

* Embalming is not permitted in the Jewish faith nor in certain others.

condition of the remains has deteriorated, the funeral home may use a metal casket, which could be hermetically sealed, thus eliminating the possibility of odor. Of course, embalming would not be necessary if direct cremation was chosen.

Preparing for the Arrangement Meeting

Prior to the arrangement meeting with the funeral director, it is helpful to consider the following items. Preparation will make the meeting easier.

If not completed during the first call, prepare a draft death announcement or funeral notice, which can be completed once you and the funeral director discuss the service.

Select clothing, jewelry, and personal effects to be worn by the deceased or displayed. Such items as war medals, family photos, awards, paintings, or poetry are commonly displayed or placed in the casket to commemorate the life of the deceased. Decide which items should be returned prior to burial.

If the deceased had been ill for a long time prior to death and had undergone tremendous physical changes, select a picture showing your loved one in healthier days. This picture can be used as a reference during the preparation of the remains.

The funeral home must complete the death certificate; determine and record vital family history relating to the deceased, such as parents' names and birthplaces, mother's maiden name, name of surviving spouse, and other important details.

Arrangement Meeting

The arrangement meeting may last anywhere from one to two hours, depending on the information required

---

and the services desired. In most cases, it is the first opportunity to meet the funeral director, so both parties should take some time to get acquainted. It is wise not to rush through the arrangements. This may lead to hasty decisions and regrets after the service, particularly in financial matters. Do not hesitate to ask any questions or provide additional information. All these things will help the funeral director to advise the family and will usually enhance the services provided.

During the meeting, the funeral director will record information on a funeral service agreement or contract. This will include identification of the deceased, his or her family history, and details about the funeral service.

In addition to a review of the professional services provided, the funeral director will also provide an explanation of the various products available. These may include caskets or other containers, urns, protective grave liners, or burial vaults. At some time during the arrangement meeting, family members are shown the products available and asked to make a selection of those required. Unless asked to leave, the funeral director will remain with the family during the selection process.

Most funeral homes will also assist the family with third-party services. These services may include: arrangements with the cemetery, clergy and musicians for the funeral, placement of radio and newspaper notices, orders of flowers, and coordination of transportation of the deceased. The funeral director welcomes the opportunity to address all third-party services for the family. Many funeral homes will also make cash advances, on behalf of the family, to cover all third-party expenses. These expenses are added to the total costs of the funeral services provided by the funeral home and itemized accordingly.

Some funeral homes complete a clothing, jewelry, and personal effects form that identifies each item provided by the family to be displayed or placed on the deceased. Special instructions are also recorded, such as which items are to be returned prior to burial.

If cremation is chosen, forms granting authorization to cremate and governing final disposition must be completed and signed.

Costs associated with each of the services provided are itemized in the funeral service contract, and the funeral director will take time to go over these costs and make every effort to work within the family's financial circumstances or budget. The funeral director will also review various financial benefits and assistance programs that may be available for survivors.

At the end of the arrangement meeting, the funeral director will review the recorded information with the person who has the legal authority to execute the various contractual agreements made. This individual may be the next-of-kin, executor, or legal representative. If the deceased had prepared a will, it is best to refer to it prior to the arrangement meeting, especially if the executor or legal representative is someone other than the immediate next-of-kin. This is most important when the funeral director must determine who is legally permitted to authorize cremation of the deceased.

The Death Announcement

During the arrangement meeting, the funeral director will need to discuss the family's wishes with respect to

---

the death announcement. For many, announcing the death of a loved one is more than just identifying the deceased and surviving family members and providing details of the funeral service. It is a way for immediate family members to express their feelings or simply bid a final farewell.

Traditionally, these short announcements appear in newspapers as "obituaries," but are referred to by funeral directors as either death or funeral notices. A more detailed account of a person's life, usually written by a newspaper or a third party on behalf of the family, is generally considered to be an obituary. Quite often when obituaries are not written, the death notice is used to elaborate upon the life of the deceased and to pay tribute.

Although every death notice contains basic elements common to all, each is different. Each family has unique expressions, language, and writing styles that personalize the way in which its members commemorate and remember their loved one.

Basic elements

The death notice is an essential link to the community and should include information to help people decide how best to support the family and pay their final respects to the deceased. The following elements are the most common and useful components of the death notice.

Identity of the deceased:
Notices in newspapers appear in alphabetical order. The surname of the deceased will appear first, followed by given names or initials. If the deceased was not well-known by a given name, a nickname may be added in

parentheses. A woman's maiden name is also placed in parentheses, if she had taken her husband's surname.

Titles, degrees, professional and political designations, or awards are also included with the name. For example, if the deceased was a university graduate and professional, the appropriate academic degree abbreviations would follow the name. Commendations or wartime contributions are also noted, for both men and women.

If the deceased worked in a particular job or business for a long period of time, or was married for many years, this level of commitment may also be noted. A notice may include a phrase such as, "served as an orderly for 40 years at a local hospital," or "devoted husband of 60 years."

Identities of the survivors:
Even though readers of the notice may not have known the deceased personally, they may be close friends of family members. A list of those who are "left to mourn the loss" or who "celebrate the life" of the deceased should be included in the notice. Generally, the immediate family is named first, starting with the surviving spouse or companion, children and their spouses, grandchildren, great-grandchildren, and, if applicable, parents and parents-in-law. If there is a large family, names of the grandchildren and great-grandchildren are not usually listed, but are specified numerically. Siblings, along with brothers- and sisters-in-law, are also named. Some notices mention nieces, nephews and close friends, especially when there is not a large immediate family. For those survivors who do not live where the funeral is being held, their place of residence is usually noted.

Quite often, a list of survivors includes predeceased relatives such as parents, children, and siblings. The years of these deaths are sometimes mentioned. On rare occasions, the names of pets or reference to a pet is included among the survivors.

Date, location, and cause of death:
Most death notices record the date and location of death but not always the cause. The cause may sometimes be implied through phrases or requests included in the notice. In addition to its importance to genealogists, the date of death may help people decide how to respond. They may visit the funeral home or attend the service if death occurred recently, but may send the family a note if death occurred some time earlier.

Hospitals, public or private nursing homes, and the home of the deceased or an immediate family member are the most common locations where death occurs. Others include death at sea, on the highway, in a cabin or country home, and while traveling. Usually, specific names of hospitals, nursing homes, and similar institutions are mentioned in the notice. Hospital treatment, such as palliative care, intensive care (ICU), and cardiac care (CCU) are also noted, along with special thanks to the nurses and doctors.

Families often personalize the final moments of a loved one's life by adding such phrases as "in the presence of her loving family at home" or "surrounded by his family." Phrases such as "passed peacefully away," "died suddenly," and "passed peacefully away, after a courageous battle with cancer" all give the reader some insight into how a person died. The mention of in memoriam donations to a foundation for the research and treatment of a particular illness may also shed light on the deceased's experiences.

Funeral service details:
The type of funeral service selected dictates how this part of the notice is written. With traditional earth burial, families may designate either special visiting hours or full-day visitation. Special hours imply that the family will only be in attendance during these hours. The visitation period will usually stretch over two to three days, followed by a religious service and interment. The dates, times, and locations of all these services will be noted.

Families who choose cremation will mention in the notice such phrases as "at his request, cremation has taken place" or "funeral services will be followed by cremation." Phrases such as a "memorial service," which is a service without the body present, or "private interment at a later date" are also used when cremation is chosen.

Donation details:
Many people like to express their support to the family in a tangible way by sending flowers, leaving sympathy or prayer cards, or giving donations in memory of the deceased. To guide the public in that regard, most families will specify that flowers are "gratefully accepted" or "in lieu of flowers, donations may be made to" a specific charity, foundation, or organization. Some families give sympathizers the option of donations to "a charity of one's choice."

Special notes:
As mentioned above, the death announcement is used by some families to bid a final farewell. This may be in

the form of a short poem, verse, or a simple phrase, such as "forever loved," "we love you, Mom," "always remembered," or "rest in peace."

Internet Obituaries

Over the past few years the internet has become a major influence on our lives. For the majority of users, it has become an instant source of information and communication. Because of this, an increasing number of funeral homes have established an on-line presence and are publishing obituaries, death notices, and tributes either by a third party or by doing it themselves on their own Web sites. Unlike local newspapers with a limited circulation, an internet tribute or notice is accessible for view globally and may be kept on-line for an extended period.

Funeral homes are also offering to accept on-line messages of condolence on behalf of the family or are inviting those people who are unable to visit the funeral home to sign their on-line guestbook. These internet services are usually mentioned at the end of the death notice that appears in the local newspaper.

A more comprehensive and insightful discussion of obituaries and death notices is contained in Mary Ellen Gillian's book *Obits: The Way We Say Goodbye,* published by Serious Publishing, 7249 Waverley Ave., Burnaby, BC, Canada, V5J 4A7. Phone: (604) 879-0321, Fax (604) 875-0007.

Chapter Five

Whose
Funeral is It, Anyway?

As many farewells as there be stars in heaven.
—William Shakespeare,
Troilus and Cressida

I n his book *Funerals and How to Improve Them*, Dr.
Tony Walter dedicates a chapter to the question.
"Whose funeral is it, anyway?" His answer is both
interesting and thought-provoking.

It is quite often said by funeral directors, spiritual
leaders, and other professionals specializing in bereavement support that a funeral is for the living, not the
dead. But it is only in the twentieth century that this
view has gained such acceptance so that now, "the funeral is performed essentially for the sake of the next-
of-kin." In earlier times, most people would have said
that the funeral was performed on behalf of the deceased.

Legally, the funeral does belong to the next-of-kin.
In your Last Will and Testament you can state, with
the force of law, what should happen to your property,
but you can state only a preference as to what should
happen to your body. If you wanted to be buried, your

spouse could still choose to cremate you instead. Once you die, your body is the property of your next-of-kin or of your estate. But philosophically the next-of-kin are not the only ones who will grieve the loss of a loved one. This point can best be illustrated by the following scenarios.

Consider a young adult male who dies as a result of his wayward life. His parents, having rejected him earlier, have not seen him in years. Such a loss is very difficult, because the parents sacrificed much to raise their son and dreamed of a bright future and then … nothing. The parents of this prodigal son seem to have a good case for arranging the kind of funeral that suits them. But if relations had really broken down between the man and his parents, is it right for the funeral to say or imply things about him that deny everything he lived for? And what about the man's girlfriend? Is she not equally traumatized? So whose funeral is it—the deceased's, the girlfriend's, or the parents'? The parents risk arranging something inappropriate while their son's girlfriend suffers silently through the service.

Then there is the common case of an elderly person, residing in a resident care facility for more than a decade, who may have become closer to the "family" of friends and staff in the facility than his or her own family. The loss felt by those at the facility may be greater than that of a biological family whom the deceased had barely seen over the past several years.

Or examine an increasingly common situation. A divorced father of two children never remarried but had a female companion. His funeral was attended not only by his children, but also by his ex-wife and his companion. The children arranged the funeral themselves and were wise to think not of what they or any of their father's past acquaintances would like, but of what he himself would have preferred. They picked poems, songs, and readings that summed up the man. Furthermore, although the children were Christians, their father was not at all religious, so they held a secular or non-religious funeral.

In his book, Dr. Walter states: "To forgo one's own beliefs and values, and arrange the kind of funeral that honours the actual life of the deceased, seems to me to acknowledge something very profound about bereavement. Losing someone involves handing them over, whereas to grasp the funeral as your own possession is to cling to your unfulfilled hopes for the deceased. Legally, the funeral belongs to the next-of-kin, but this is one occasion when people would be wise not to stand too firmly by their rights."

Group Representation

When arranging a funeral, survivors would do well to keep in mind those groups or organizations who were connected to the deceased. "Funerals belong not only to the deceased and to the next-of-kin, they also belong to groups. The tighter knit the group, or the more threatened it is by death, the more likely it will take over the funeral. It is to restate its values at the funeral if it is to survive," says Dr. Walter.

For example, a soldier on a peacekeeping mission dies and his body is flown home to his family. The soldier is given a full military funeral. During the funeral service, the soldier's cap and the flag of the nation he served are placed on the casket. At the burial, guns are raised and rounds fired in salute. This funeral is not a

---

symbol of the grief of the soldier's parents. It does not reflect his unique personality. It is a ceremony that powerfully reaffirms military values.

When a firefighter, police officer, emergency medical technician, or anyone who risks his or her life for others dies, a funeral similar to the military service will prevail, unless the family specifically requests otherwise. When a member of a group dies, his or her colleagues have to turn out in force, not only to pay their respects to their friend, but also to reaffirm their respect for one another.

As Dr. Walter says:

> *The values of the group must be asserted to be more powerful than the pain of the individual. Solidarity between the survivors must be shown. As individuals, they may not come to the same answers, but there is comfort in facing the questions together, in knowing that the group goes on even as individuals go to pieces. This power of the group to heal its bereaved members exists whenever the deceased was a member of an ongoing community. It is why, apart from any religious faith, there is usually something extra at the funeral of a regular member of a church. The mourners share their loss and reaffirm what they, as a group, believe in, even at a time when, as individuals, they may never have had more serious doubts.*

Often, the main group to which the deceased belongs is his or her family. Expressed then are usually the values common to many families. Loyalty, kindness, hospitality, and faithfulness are featured in the eulogies at the funeral service.

In a mobile society, there are also those who knew the deceased, but are not members of the family or of any close-knit group to which he or she belonged. Often, the numbers of such people turning up for a funeral are not anticipated by the family.

A person's circle of friends and acquaintances can be wide and varied, so that it may be some weeks before everyone hears of the death. This is why, among mobile professional people, memorial services are sometimes performed some weeks after the death. For those who may not wish to travel, the sending of memorial cards and written letters of sympathy become the ritual through which the person is honored and remembered.

Dr. Walter offers this thought: "Ultimately, the funeral is performed not just for the deceased, nor the family, nor the community, nor for friends. But the death of a human being must be marked. The funeral belongs to humanity."

Chapter Six
Choices to Be Made

For tho' from out of bourne of Time and Place
The flood may bear me far,
I hope to see my Pilot face to face
When I have crost the bar.
　　　　—Alfred Lord Tennyson, *Crossing the Bar*

Often the most difficult and emotional part of funeral arrangements is the selection of a casket. Because of this, many people are reluctant to spend much time in the selection room or to ask any questions about the merchandise they are about to purchase. Unfortunately, a short time after the funeral service, some family members experience feelings of doubt or regret about the casket chosen. They may ask themselves: "Why did we select such an expensive casket? Will it provide adequate protection for the remains? Did we get good value for the money we spent?"

The purchase of a casket is unlike any other purchase one might make. It is very personal and, in many ways, reflects the family members' myriad feelings for the deceased. Trying to balance these emotions while selecting the "right" casket can be a challenge. One way in which family members may become more comfortable with their purchase decisions when the time comes is to learn more about available options well in advance. This chapter allows readers to examine the current products available, so that they can make sound decisions when faced with this very difficult decision.

Generally, a person making funeral arrangements may select from a group of 10 to 25 caskets ranging in price from several hundred to several thousand dollars. Caskets will vary in price according to the materials from which they are made, the quality of the workmanship, the grade of the interior fabric, and the special features provided. Take time to have the funeral director explain the different types and features available.

Types of Caskets

Traditionally, there are two types of caskets used in most funeral services: wood and metal. There are various types of woods and metals from which to choose however. Wooden caskets range from a basic, embossed, cloth-covered plywood to solid hardwoods. Wood laminates with polished finishes are also available. Metal or protective caskets, designed to resist the entrance of air and water, are constructed from solid steel, stainless steel, copper, or bronze.

The most expensive **wooden caskets** are made from solid hardwoods. A hardwood comes from such leaf-bearing trees as mahogany, walnut, cherry, maple, pecan, oak, and poplar. A softwood comes from needle- and cone-bearing trees. Technically, pine is a softwood, but a pine casket is commonly considered to be a hardwood casket.

As with furniture, the type of wood used affects both appearance and cost of the casket. Depending on the size and style of the casket, between 150 and 225 board feet of solid lumber are used in its construction. Many hardwood caskets are created in the same tradition as fine furniture, with the wood's natural features enhanced by the use of intricate, hand-carved details, multiple sandings, and hand-rubbed finishes.

The next level below hardwood caskets are those made from wood laminates. These are plywood caskets with hardwood strips laminated or glued to the surface of the plywood. The laminate material is then sanded and polished, creating a satin or gloss finish.

The most inexpensive wood caskets available are cloth-covered. These are usually made of plywood or pressboard covered with an embossed cloth that comes in a variety of colors.

The most common **metal caskets** are made from steel. It was not until the twentieth century that Batesville Casket Co. of Indiana started mass producing the first protective steel caskets. Steel caskets feature a one-piece top formed by a single sheet of steel, which offers superior strength. The bottom is welded into each casket using a continuous weld along the entire seam. This ensures a seal that air, water, or any other element found in the soil cannot penetrate.

In most casket selection rooms, the funeral director will show various styles of steel caskets, with a designated gauge. The gauge measures the casket's wall thickness or the thickness of the sheet metal used in its construction. The lower the gauge, the thicker the steel. For example, the wall thickness of an 18-gauge casket is more than that of a 20-gauge model.

Stainless steel caskets are constructed from two grades of stainless steel: series 300, containing corrosion-resistant chromium and nickel, and series 400, which has no nickel, but is protected by a cathodic protection system. Cathodic protection is a method of retarding corrosion on the outer surfaces of all carbon steel and series 400 stainless steel. A bar made of a special magnesium alloy is installed in a channel formed into the bottom of each casket. Should a corrosion-producing condition occur, the alloy stimulates an electro-chemical reaction, which helps protect the casket from damage. When the corrosive condition ceases, the system becomes inactive. The same type of protection is used to protect pipelines and holds of ocean-going vessels.

In addition to cathodic protection, each metal casket is equipped with a one-piece, solid rubber gasket. This gasket forms a highly effective seal between the top and bottom of the casket. When screwed shut, each metal casket is hermetically or vacuum-sealed.

Batesville was also the first casket manufacturer to mass produce bronze and copper caskets. Both bronze and copper are completely safe from rust.

Casket Features

Other notable features incorporated in selected hardwood and metal caskets include:

- An interior liner, which is leak-proof and puncture resistant.
- A lift-and-tilt bed mechanism, which helps achieve an ideal viewing height.

- A memorial record system that allows families to put personal notes into a small Plexiglas™ capsule, which screws into the side of the casket.
- A Living Memorial Program™ where the casket manufacturer plants a tree seedling in memory of a loved one.
- A Memory Safe™, which is a removable drawer located in the foot-cap panel on most of their premium hardwood caskets. This feature allows families to secure and display photos, letters, medals, and other mementos inside the casket. The drawer may be left open during the visitation to display items to mourners and allow them to add their own tokens, or it may be kept closed for private keepsakes.
- Lifesymbol™ Corners, which are interchangeable corners that give family members the chance to personalize a casket by selecting a style that holds a special meaning for them or the deceased. There are more than a dozen styles available including praying hands, a lighthouse, fish, Masonic emblem, or a single rose. All corners are attached with an easy, one-bolt fastener.

The York Group of Houston, Texas, the second largest casket manufacturer in North America, recently introduced the "Expressions" casket, which features a special coating on which you can write a final farewell. Made of solid ash hardwood, each casket has a glossy, pearly finish and comes with a set of permanent markers. Once written on the casket surface, the message will not come off.

Burial Vaults and Protective Liners

A **burial vault** is a sealed outer container into which a casket is placed prior to its underground interment or burial in a cemetery. It provides added protection for both the casket and the deceased, particularly where there are poor soil conditions and high groundwater levels. It will also support the weight of the earth and any heavy equipment that may pass over the grave, thus substantially reducing problems at the graveside and, in turn, cemetery costs.

There are many types of vaults available. Some are elaborately designed with high-quality structural concrete cores and reinforced interiors and exteriors made of high-impact plastics, stainless steel, bronze, or copper. The concrete vault covers may also be encased in bronze and copper and include other features, such as special emblems, accent bars, and nameplates.

Vault construction

Concrete burial vaults weigh between 2,200 and 2,700 pounds and are designed to support loads exceeding 25,000 pounds. A typical vault is made of a strong, reinforced concrete casing chemically bonded to a tough, seamless plastic lining. To increase its load bearing capacity, some manufacturers use ribbed liners. The strength and durability of a concrete vault is enhanced by the use of additional metal liners of either bronze, copper, or stainless steel. For superior strength, an outer casing of bronze or stainless steel is also used.

The most important structural component of the concrete vault is its cover. To help support the tremendous forces, additional reinforcement is used. Its shape is also important as it is designed to distribute the loads evenly over the vault surface. To ensure that the vault is water-resistant once the cover is attached, a thick rubber membrane is placed in the groove between the base and cover.

An alternative to the heavy concrete vault is the steel vault. Still popular in many cemeteries, steel vaults are quite different from their concrete counterparts. The primary difference is the manner in which the casket is placed inside the vault. In the steel vault, the casket slides inside through the end of the unit. A hinged door is then closed and secured tightly by turning a single bolt. A rubber membrane separates the steel door from the sides, and once the bolt is fully turned, the vault is hermetically sealed. All other joints are welded. The exterior of the vault is usually gold in color.

The lightest of the three vaults is the fiberglass unit, which is white and weighs about 130 pounds. It consists of a bottom piece, upon which the casket is placed, and a reinforced upper dome that fits over the casket. When the two pieces are fitted together, the surface contact points are sealed with a butyl rubber tape to keep out moisture.

Both the steel and fiberglass vaults have approximately the same dimensions as the concrete vault and can also accommodate all standard caskets.

Graveside

The burial vault is usually delivered to the cemetery on the day of the service. Because of its extreme weight, the concrete vault is placed by mechanical means on a specifically designed lowering device. Once the grave-

---

Chapter Six Choices to be Made

side service is completed and the family departs, the casket is sealed inside the vault while it is above ground. It is then gently lowered into the grave.

In contrast, the lighter steel vault and bottom of the fiberglass unit are placed manually on the lowering device. Upon arrival at graveside, the casket is put in or on the vault prior to the committal service. Unless otherwise requested, each vault will be secured and lowered into the grave after the family's departure.

Protective liners

Most cemeteries prefer that the casket be placed in some type of outer receptacle at the time of burial. Unless the use of a concrete or steel vault is mandatory, the container most often used is a wooden shell with cover. It is commonly referred to by funeral directors as a "protective liner."

Although this liner does not provide any structural support or protection for the casket once the grave is backfilled, it does support the sides of the grave when it is opened, particularly during inclement weather. It also improves the grave's appearance and shields the casket from large rocks and gravel during the closing of the grave.

Chapter Seven

The Traditional Funeral

Let no one pay me honor with tears,
nor celebrate my funeral rites with weeping.
— Quintus Ennius, *Cicero, De Secectute*

Many families choose what is commonly referred to in the profession as the "traditional" or "full" funeral service. This service is subdivided into four specific segments, namely:

- A period of visitation or wake in a funeral home usually lasting for two or three days and where the deceased rests in an open or closed casket.
- A public or private ceremony in a funeral home chapel or place of worship of one's choice.
- Committal service and burial or entombment in a cemetery or mausoleum.
- Memorialization or the placement of some type of permanent marker or inscription at the burial site.

The Visitation
Many funeral services include a period of visitation or a wake, with the deceased in an open or closed casket and

often resting in one of the reposing rooms at the funeral home. It is during this time that relatives and friends gather with the immediate family, in the presence of the remains, to extend their sympathy and comfort during the period of bereavement.

Most families choose to view the remains of their loved one, if it is at all possible. The family should view the deceased for the first time in privacy. Generally, a family will be advised to come to the funeral home approximately a half-hour before public visitation. At this time, the funeral director will meet family members and escort them to the room in which the casket has been placed.

After leading the family to the visitation room, the funeral director will respond to any last-minute changes the family may wish to make. After tending to the family's needs, funeral directors leave the family members alone in the visitation room so they can have a private moment with their loved one. The public is not permitted to enter until the family members have advised the funeral director that they are ready to commence visitation.

During visitation, the funeral director will be available but would generally go unnoticed. The funeral director periodically brings in floral arrangements and ensures that these arrangements are appropriately placed with the least possible interruption. Otherwise, the funeral director's job at this stage is to respond to a family's needs.

The maximum period of visitation at most funeral homes is 12 hours per day, beginning at 10 a.m. and ending at 10 p.m. Visitation may start any time within this period. Mourners may also be encouraged to visit during specified hours, such as from 2 to 4 p.m. or 7 to 9 p.m., when members of the family are there to meet relatives and friends.

Children at a Funeral Home

Children experience grief just as adults do. It is important to remember, however, that children deal with death differently at different ages, and their reactions are not always obvious or immediate. Some children mature faster than others. The level of a child's emotional development should be taken into consideration by an adult before talking to a child about death or bringing that child to a funeral home for a wake or service.

From the funeral director's perspective, no restrictions are placed on the family. The final decision to bring young children to the funeral home is always the family's to make and will depend on the children and the circumstances. Nevertheless, the funeral director can assist those adults willing to talk openly to their child or children about the death of a loved one. There are some wonderful resource materials available for both children and adults relating to the death of a parent, grandparent, special relative, or friend that the funeral director can provide or recommend. Some of these include coloring books for children, depicting the various stages of a funeral, or brochures for adults that answer a child's questions about death. The animated musical video *Charlotte's Web*, a story of the miracles of birth, friendship, and death, also provides children with exceptional insight into some of life's mysteries.

In all circumstances, children need adults to confirm that it's all right to be sad and to cry and that the hurt they feel now won't last forever.

The Funeral Service

A funeral service is a ceremony during which relatives, friends, and associates pay respect to the deceased and comfort the survivors. Regardless of religious affiliation, it is customary to hold a funeral service as a means of giving testimony to a life that was lived. For those who are religious, the service is a spiritual occasion, usually conducted in a place of worship or funeral home chapel with a priest, rabbi, or other spirtual leader officiating. Others may choose a "humanistic" or secular service.

The scheduling of a religious service will depend upon the schedule of the celebrant. The funeral director will look into such schedules shortly after the arrangement meeting. In general, Roman Catholic services are held in the morning, while other Christian and non-Christian religions will hold services at any time of day.

The service is often designed by the family in consultation with the celebrant, funeral director, and members of fraternal, military, or other organizations previously affiliated with the deceased. The career or profession of the deceased may also be a part of the service. For instance, if the deceased had been a member of the police or fire department, fellow members usually attend the service in full uniform, while some may serve as pallbearers or an honor guard.

The type of hymns, songs, and music selected for the service is another way in which a family may pay tribute to a loved one. It is not uncommon to see youth or adult choirs, bands, guest soloists, or musicians in attendance. Music can be a very special component in this service of thanksgiving and celebration.

Some families may also elect to have a personalized bulletin printed and distributed at the church or chapel outlining the order of service along with hymns, poems, or any other script that had special meaning to the deceased.

To prepare for the funeral service, the funeral director will arrive at the place of worship or chapel 30 to 45 minutes before it is scheduled to start. Preparations may include the placement of flowers at the altar, coordination of the pallbearers and others participating in the service, and greeting family members and friends. Most important, the funeral director is there to answer questions and tend to last-minute details, thus supporting the grieving family.

The Committal Service

The final segment of the funeral is the committal service, conducted at graveside or the crematorium. It may be either public or private.

In the case of a traditional funeral with earth burial, the committal service will take place directly following the service at the church or chapel. The easiest, most orderly way to get from the site of the service to the cemetery is by a procession. Therefore, the funeral procession remains an integral part of the funeral.

Immediate family members, other relatives, close friends, and, where applicable, representatives from organizations in which the deceased was affiliated proceed to the cemetery, led by the funeral director and celebrant. To maintain its integrity and dignity, the route of the funeral procession is planned by the funeral director. On occasion, it may include driving past the residence, place of business, or another special place in the life of the deceased.

Earlier on the day of the service, the gravesite is prepared. Preparation usually consists of the placement of a protective grave liner or burial vault, grass matting, a lowering device, chairs, and a canopy. Upon arrival at graveside, the funeral director, clergy, family, and friends will gather around the final resting place of the deceased as the pallbearers place the casket on the lowering device.

Prior to the service, the family will have chosen between lowering the casket into the grave, partially lowering it so the top of the casket is at ground level, or not lowering it until the family leaves the cemetery. There are varying opinions about this practice, and it would certainly be prudent to speak to both the funeral director and celebrant before making a choice. Partial lowering has become the accepted practice, however.

Once the casket and mourners are in position, the celebrant will commence a short committal service. Beginning with scripture readings or prayers, the celebrant will then formally commit the deceased to the earth. During the committal service for a Roman Catholic, the priest will sprinkle holy water over the casket and ground, symbolizing the consecration of the grave. In this case, the casket is not lowered until this is done. For other Christian denominations, the funeral director may sprinkle sand over the casket as a symbol of the phrase "earth to earth, ashes to ashes and dust to dust." The casket may be lowered or remain stationary during the sprinkling of the sand. It is traditional at a Jewish graveside service once the casket is lowered to the bottom of the grave for some of those in attendance to place shovels of earth over the casket.

Following the celebrant's remarks, representatives of other organizations or groups are given the opportunity to pay tribute to the deceased. Each have their own rites and rituals, which are performed with dignity and out of respect for the deceased.

After the committal service, the funeral director will see to the needs of the family and then drive the celebrant back to the place of worship. The celebrant may also attend the repast or family reception. It is only after all mourners have departed that the graveside equipment is removed and the grave closed.

When cremation is chosen, some Protestant denominations prefer to have what is known as a "committal to the flame." In this case, the clergy will be present at the crematory just prior to the placement of the deceased in the crematorium by the funeral director. A short service is conducted, followed by cremation. Family members may or may not choose to attend. Following cremation, if the cremated remains are to be interred, the interment will also be preceded by a committal service similar to that mentioned above.

In *The Funeral and the Mourners*, Paul E. Irion writes: "The committal service provides, as nothing else does so graphically, a symbolic demonstration that the kind of relationship which has existed between mourners and the deceased is now at an end."

Mausoleum Entombment

Despite the fact that mausoleum entombment has long been considered one of the world's finest and most dignified forms of burial, most people know very little about it. Entombment is the interment of human remains in a tomb or crypt. Today, it is most often referred to as above-ground interment. Casketed remains are placed in a crypt or individual compartment within a mausoleum, which is then sealed with a granite or marble front.

Historically, the word *mausoleum* comes from the large temple-like structure that served as a final resting place for King Mausolus, who died in 353 B.C. Erected in the ancient Asia Minor city of Halicarnassus by Queen Artemisia, the mausoleum was one of the Seven Wonders of the Ancient World.

Today, an indoor community mausoleum is simply a large building designed to provide above-ground interment or entombment for a number of unrelated people. There are also outdoor or garden community mausoleums and family mausoleums, which are relatively small, privately owned structures designed to house the remains of individual families.

Sharing the costs of the mausoleum with other individuals has made it more affordable. For example, depending on its location within the building or structure, the cost of a single crypt may range from $3,500 to more than $10,000. Double and family crypts are also available.

Memorialization

Memorialization has become an established custom through the centuries. It involves the placement of some sort of permanent marker or inscription at the place of burial or in some other special place, such as a church.

A memorial celebrates a life which has been lived. It can take many forms. In a cemetery, the most common memorials are upright monuments or headstones of granite or marble, or flat markers of bronze set flush with the ground. Each contains the name of the deceased and, in many cases, the dates of birth and death. Some headstones and markers may be manufactured in a particular shape, such as a heart, or include a short verse, phrase, picture, or symbol providing the visitor with a small clue about the deceased and how survivors felt about him or her. The sizes of memorials are regulated in most urban cemeteries with some restrictions found in rural locations.

Some families choose companion headstones or markers with sufficient space to record the names and particulars of each spouse. Others use inscriptions on mausoleum walls. For those families who choose cremation, memorialization may consist of an inscription of a loved one's name on the walls or niches of columbaria or structures that hold the urns of cremated remains.

The way in which we pay tribute to the life of a person is not restricted solely to cemeteries. In churches and synagogues, we find many wonderful examples of memorials dedicated to those who have gone before us. For example, most of the older, historic churches have bronze, wooden, or granite plaques containing the names of those persons who made the "supreme sacrifice" in both World Wars and other conflicts.

Churches are filled with stained-glass windows that have been placed there by parishioners in memory of their loved ones. Bulletins, prayer books, bibles, and flowers are other items that are often given to the church in someone's memory.

In fact, many churches and synagogues have been built or completed major projects because of people's desire to memorialize or remember. Donations to a memorial building or organ fund are commonplace in the church community. Memorial endowment funds or funds whose principal must be maintained with only the investment income used have also been established by churches and synagogues thanks to the generosity of parishioners in whose memory monies have been left or given.

To the funeral director, a funeral service is the supreme act of memorialization. It is a time to remember, celebrate, or pay tribute to the life of the deceased. Many of the services provided by the funeral home are designed to help the family memorialize their loved one. In the early stages of the funeral arrangement meeting, the funeral director will ask a number of questions to complete essential documentation. Yet, some are asked simply to get to know more about the deceased. People love to relate favorite stories or talk about those persons they love. That's memorialization, too.

As another form of memorialization, any tangible items that were important to the deceased can be displayed during visitation or other times during the funeral service. Items such as medals, photographs, paintings, plaques, poems, and cards are often displayed. Many funeral homes have additional furnishings available, such as pedestals, pillows, easels, and tables on which to display these items for the family. Some families choose to place special mementos in the casket or urn with the deceased. Each item reflects the family's desire to memorialize their loved one.

Another area commonly used by families to memorialize is the funeral notice. In some cases, these notices serve as final words of farewell and are often the way survivors pay tribute. Newspapers will also print obituaries or a brief account of the life of the deceased.

Memorialization can take many forms. The choices are limited only by the imagination.

Military Funerals

The provision of Military Funeral Honors is a way in which a nation shows its deep gratitude to those who, in times of war and peace, have faithfully defended their country. It is the final act of respect that a grateful nation can provide to a veteran's family.

A few years ago the U.S. Department of Defense initiated a new program to improve the provision of Military Funeral Honors to eligible veterans. Historically, funeral honors were provided when resources were available to do so. The new program, appropriately named "Honoring Those Who Served," by law now mandates the provision of Military Funeral Honors to all requests for eligible veterans' funerals.

The basic Military Funeral Honors ceremony consists of three core elements: folding and presentation of the American flag to the next-of-kin, and the playing of "Taps," the bugle call that became mandatory at military funeral ceremonies in 1891. The ceremony is performed by an Honor Guard detail consisting of not less than two members of the military branch in which the deceased veteran served. One member of the detail shall be representative of the parent Service of the deceased veteran. Depending on the culture and traditions of the Service, additional personnel or other elements of funeral honors may be added.

Military Funeral Honors are provided by the Department of Defense at no cost to the family. The funeral director will contact the appropriate Service representative for the region. Requests for funeral honors are based on the final interment site location, not the funeral service location, if they are different. If there is no final disposition site, the ceremony may be held at the location of the memorial service. At least 48 hours notice is required by the Services in order to organize the funeral honors detail.

Eligibility for Military Funeral Honors

The following are eligible for Military Funeral Honors:

- Military members on active duty
- Military retirees
- Members and former members of the Selected Reserve
- Eligible U.S. veterans of any war
- Other U.S. veterans who served at least one term of enlistment and separated under conditions other than dishonorable.

For more information about establishing a veteran's eligibility or obtaining a copy of Discharge documents, contact National Personnel Records Center or access the information via the Internet at www.nara.gov/publications/forms/sf180a.pdf.

Burial at sea services in the United States are offered by the Department of the Navy for members on active duty, retirees, and honorably discharged veterans of all branches of the U.S. Military. Also eligible are U.S. civilian marine personnel of the Military Sealift command and dependents of members, retirees, and veterans of the uniformed services. Services are performed on Navy vessels deployed on official maneuvers. Therefore, it is not possible for family members to be present. The family will be notified by the commanding officer of the vessel and the date, time, longitude, and latitude of the committal service.

To initiate a burial at sea, a Burial at Sea Request/ Authorization Form must be completed and signed by the immediate next of kin, executor, or person legally responsible for arranging the final disposition.

Because the remains may be held for long periods until a ship is scheduled to get underway, the deceased must be completely embalmed and preserved for at least 60 days. A metal casket is also required, and it must be banded, weighted, and a specific number of holes drilled into each of its sides. A diagram describing the procedure is available from the Navy Ports of embarkation, including Norfolk, Virginia; Jacksonville, Florida; and Corpus Christi, Texas on the Atlantic side and San Diego, California; Bremerton, Washington; and Hawaii on the Pacific.

For more information about burial at sea services and procedures, you may call 1-800-647-6676 (Ext. 628 or 629).

Celebration Rituals

A funeral is a series of rituals and traditions that is influenced by our social, religious, and cultural values and beliefs. While striving to plan a more personal and meaningful funeral, increasing numbers of families are choosing alternative funeral practices. To keep pace with change and satisfy emotional needs, religious communities and family members are creating new rituals and traditions.

Between the years 1946 and 1964, a population explosion produced the largest generation in the history of the world. Now in their 40s and 50s, the "Baby Boom" generation has had a significant impact on society's values and beliefs, and as such is reshaping the death-care industry. Baby boomers are reinventing the funeral. They want to take an active part in funeral arrangements and do so by many means, including the selection of personal effects for display, unconventional eulogies and tributes, and in developing new rituals to assist them in their time of grief and enhance the celebration and remembrance of their loved one's life.

Some of these new rituals are simply more comprehensive versions of older ones; some have been invented to fill a need by the family and community to share in the celebration of the life of the deceased. Whether to reflect something of the life of the person commemorated, or to allow a larger community to participate in the marking of the loved one's passing, the rituals and traditions associated with funerals are vitally important to the processes of mourning and healing.

Emerging trends such as cremation, preplanning, alternative services, and innovative merchandising and products, combined with consumers' demand for quality service and value, has caused funeral directors to refocus on value-added services rather than simply providing a casket and facility.

Personalizing a Funeral Service

Personalizing a funeral service can be a very rewarding and fulfilling experience for family members. It focuses the thoughts of those who participate on the person whose life they wish to celebrate and honor, and in doing so begins the healing process. There are a variety of ways in which a service can be personalized, from simply displaying personal items during the viewing, to altering traditional forms of services.

Some examples of ways in which a service may be personalized include:

- Pictures: these may be displayed individually or placed in an album. Many funeral homes provide memory boards, where photos can be mounted and displayed.
- Memorabilia: items relevant to the life of the deceased may be used for decoration; for example, at a sea captain's funeral, his journal, captain's hat, and the bell from his ship could be displayed.
- Music: the deceased's favorite song might be played during the service; if the person was a musician, their favorite instrument might be displayed or played by a friend or loved one.
- Tributes: during the eulogy or tributes there is much opportunity for participants to speak of their loved one and share special memories and stories.
- Community Participation: if the deceased was a member of a particular community organization or fraternal group, attending members may choose to display an emblem or wear a sash or other representative article to show their respect and support.

These are a few suggestions on ways to personalize a service so that it will have greater meaning to the family, and be representative of the deceased person's life and interests. Families should consult with their funeral director, to develop suitable additions or enhancements to the service, to better celebrate the life of their loved one.

Variations to an already established ritual can also be made. Traditionally, at a graveside committal service, the funeral director will sprinkle sand over the casket or urn while the celebrant says "earth to earth, ashes to ashes, dust to dust." At the request of family members, the traditional sand may be replaced by a handful of earth or sand from the deceased's birthplace or from a place dear to that person. In this way, a new and meaningful ritual emerges from tradition, providing an important emotional connection for the family and other participants.

Different belief systems have different traditions and religious laws regarding funeral services and the disposition of the remains. Families, in consultation with both their funeral director and a member of their clergy, should be able to develop a service that honors their beliefs and the life of their loved one.

Chapter Eight
The Cremation Service

We, too, have our religion, and it is this:
Help for the living, hope for the dead.
— Robert Green Ingersoll,
Address at a Child's Grave

W hy choose cremation as opposed to a traditional burial? Some of the reasons that a greater number of people are now choosing cremation include:

- A fear of entombment or burial.
- A desire to be buried in a previously occupied family plot with a spouse, child, or parents.
- A choice not to be viewed.
- A tendency to be sensitive to the environment.
- A wish for a more simple funeral service.

It is believed, however, that the primary reason many choose cremation over burial is related to the costs involved. Many individuals or families choose cremation to save money, assuming that it is a less expensive alternative. This may or may not be true, however, depending on the type of service chosen.

For example, if the only change from a traditional service is cremation rather than earth burial, the average cost of professional services may actually increase to accommodate the cost of cremation and the purchase of a simple hardwood urn. The average cemetery costs could decrease, however, if the urn is interred in a previously occupied family plot.

On the other hand, if direct cremation is chosen with a memorial service and interment of a hardwood urn in a previously occupied family plot, the average cost will be less than a traditional service. Again, should a family choose to scatter the cremated remains, the total cost will be further reduced.

Statistics show more and more families are asking about or choosing cremation. In the U.S., the cremation rate has grown from about 5 percent in 1970 to the current national average of approximately 28 percent. With more than 2.3 million deaths each year in the U.S., this means at least 650,000 have chosen cremation.

If it is your choice or the choice of a family member, this chapter may help provide a better understanding of the cremation process and the many services available.

Cremation Defined

Cremation is a technical heating process, which reduces the human body to its basic elements, primarily bone particles and fragments, collectively referred to as "cremated remains." The cremation process begins with the placement of the casket or container into the cremation chamber where it is subjected to intense heat and flame, reaching temperatures as high as 1800 degrees Fahrenheit.

The time to complete a cremation varies with the size and weight of the deceased, but usually takes between two and three hours. This is followed by a cooling period of about five to six hours. The basic elements remaining after cremation also depend upon the dimensions of the deceased, but generally weigh between four and eight pounds. Following the cooling period, the remains are swept or raked from the cremation chamber. Once separated from any non-combustible materials, the bone fragments may be further reduced to uniform particles for placement in an urn or similar sturdy container.

Authorization to Cremate

When an individual or family chooses cremation, certain documentation must be completed. These documents protect the crematory from liability and make clear to everyone involved the various aspects of the cremation process.

In the U.S., crematories require a Death Certificate, Burial Transit Permit and a signed "authority to cremate" document before cremation can take place. Burial Transit Permits are issued by Vital Statistics. On weekends, holidays, after-hours business, and in emergency situations only, this function is provided by the Medical Examiner or Coroner's Office.

A form authorizing the cremation of the deceased must be completed and signed by the authorized next-of-kin or the deceased's legal representative. The Authorization to Cremate form is an extremely important legal document and funeral directors should take care to ensure it is fully understood by the authorizing agent. If a death comes under the authority of the Coroner or

Medical Examiner, the Coroner or Medical Examiner must also authorize cremation.

If cremation is to be performed outside a community by another funeral home, the local funeral director with whom the initial arrangements are made must also complete and sign a Funeral Director's Certification Form. This form certifies that the person authorizing the cremation was fully advised of all the particulars associated with the Authorization to Cremate.

The Authorization to Cremate form may consist of one page or multiple pages, depending on the amount of information a particular crematory feels the consumer should have in order to fully comprehend the procedure being authorized. The form may be supplemented with additional printed material and a verbal explanation of the various aspects of cremation.

In general terms, however, the Authorization to Cremate form covers the following topics:

- Whether or not the death resulted from infectious or contagious disease.
- Whether or not embalming of the deceased is required.
- A description of the cremation process, beginning with the placement of the casket or container in the cremation chamber, the temperature achieved, procedures followed during cremation, description of the cremated remains, their removal, and final processing.
- An explanation that, due to the nature of the cremation process, any valuable material, including gold, will either be destroyed or not recoverable.

- An explanation that the deceased is always cremated in the casket or container used or received by the crematory. Most crematories require the deceased to be cremated in a combustible, leakproof, rigid, covered container, if a casket is not being used.
- Confirmation that the deceased did not have a heart pacemaker implanted, radiation-producing implant device, or any other device that could be explosive. Should such a device exist, the funeral director would be authorized to remove it.
- Confirmation that the deceased did not execute a consent allowing his or her remains, or parts thereof, to be used after death for therapeutic purposes, medical education, or scientific research, or that such consent, if executed, has been acted upon.
- Standard indemnification clause holding the crematory, its officers, and employees harmless from any liability, costs, expenses, or claims by any person arising from the matters authorized.

It is important for the person authorizing the cremation to study the form or other materials that may be provided by the funeral director so that he or she fully understands the cremation process and associated procedures that lead to the placement of cremated remains in an urn or container for final disposition.

Who Has Authority?

In certain states, legislation has been introduced allowing people to authorize their own cremation. As many other states do not permit this practice, it is recommended you confirm with the crematory authority whether authorizing your own cremation is permitted in your state.

In states where self-authorization is not permitted, once you die, your body becomes the property of your estate. The executor, next-of-kin, or legally authorized person then has the authority to choose the type of funeral service they desire for you, if not otherwise specified. This includes cremation. If this is a source of concern, take comfort in the fact that very few people change the wishes of those who take the time to record the type of funeral services they would like, such as in a will or preplanning agreement.

In most cases, the immediate next-of-kin has the authority to authorize cremation. Legally, the following qualify as next-of-kin and are listed according to priority:

- The spouse of the deceased
- The child or children of the deceased
- The grandchild or grandchildren of the deceased
- The parent(s) or legal guardian(s) of the deceased
- Sibling(s) of the deceased
- Niece(s) and nephew(s) of the deceased
- Grand-niece(s) and grand-nephew(s) of the deceased
- Grandparents of the deceased
- Aunt(s) and Uncle(s) of the deceased
- First cousin(s) of the deceased
- All persons within the same degree of kinship

- The parent(s) or legal guardian(s) of the deceased
- Siblings of the deceased

In the absence of any of these individuals, the person who would have the legal authority to authorize cremation would have to be determined, but would usually be some other relative.

In a case where the deceased left specific instructions, such as in a will, the executor of that will would have the legal authority and obligation to carry out the directions as specified. This executor would have ultimate authority, even if there were surviving next-of-kin. In cases such as these, the funeral director may ask for a copy of the portion of the deceased's will that names the executor along with a photo ID such as a driver's license to confirm the individual's identity.

Without an up-to-date will or other binding document, the line of authority may not be so clear. For example, consider the death of an individual who had been separated from his wife and living with another woman for many years but was never legally divorced. The question arises as to whether the estranged wife had the authority to authorize his cremation. Add to this the emotions of the surviving children and siblings, and the determination of legal authority is not an easy task. In cases such as these, the advice of a lawyer is often sought.

If cremation is your final wish, or you have consented to act as executor for someone who has specified cremation, take time to learn more about what is involved along with any legal responsibilities.

Chapter Nine

Options When Choosing Cremation

A journey of a thousand miles must begin with a single step.
—Lao-tzu, *The Way of Lao-tzu*

L et's consider the following question. If cremation is just one method of preparing the deceased for committal and final disposition, must a cremation service differ from that of a traditional service with viewing and a church or chapel service? The answer is no. Cremation does not prevent family, relatives, and friends from participating in the ceremonies and services of a traditional funeral. In fact, any type of service provides an outlet for the family's expression of grief and loss, and allows friends and family to demonstrate their support.

Those who choose direct cremation with no viewing may not realize the impact this decision may have on some family members, particularly those not present during the time of death or younger children and grandchildren who need that time of viewing to say goodbye. By acknowledging and seeing that death has occurred, one takes the first step in the healing process. A funeral service allows this to happen.

Nevertheless, each set of circumstances will differ and, therefore, the extent of a cremation service may be as elaborate or simple as a family desires. One point is certain, there are many options available if cremation is chosen. These may include:

- Visitation with the urn present.
- Services in a church or chapel with the urn present.
- Memorial service after cremation.
- Transportation of the cremated remains for final committal in another country.
- Delay in final committal to allow for bad weather or arrival of family.
- Interment of cremated remains in a previously occupied family plot or special section designated by the cemetery.
- Placement of the cremated remains in an interior or exterior columbarium, a structure with niches specifically designed to house urns.
- Scattering of cremated remains on land or water.

Cremation Caskets

Cremation caskets are simpler in design than those used for earth burial and are constructed specifically for cremation. In fact, some manufacturers actually refer to them as "environmentally friendly," since they are made primarily of wood with little or no metal components. As a result, they are typically less expensive than traditional caskets, yet they are crafted with the same quality.

Instead of purchasing a casket, many funeral homes offer rental caskets. They look similar to traditional caskets with one small difference—the interior lining is attached with Velcro™ and is removed and destroyed after each use. After visitation or a church or chapel service, the deceased is removed from the rental casket and placed in a cremation container. This is a rigid wooden container with cover designed specifically for direct cremation. In addition to the interior lining, the pillow and mattress board are also removed from the rental casket and placed in the cremation unit with the deceased. There are also several other types of cremation containers available that are constructed of plywood, press board, or cardboard. These containers are not designed to accommodate viewing of the deceased.

Direct Cremation

Direct cremation is cremation without any preparation and public viewing. It is simply the removal of the remains from the place of death, and placement of the remains in a casket or cremation container followed by the cremation process. The standard of care in many funeral homes is to have the remains positively identified by a family member or authorized party familiar with the deceased prior to cremation. Although not embalmed, the remains are washed, dressed, and placed in a modest cremation container designed for this purpose.

If identification or short-term viewing is not necessary and unless requested by the family, the deceased will not be dressed but instead be cremated as received from the place of death either in a hospital garment or wrapped in a blanket or linen sheet.

Unless there is a religious requirement for a short committal prayer or ritual prior to cremation, the cremation process will take place whenever it is convenient

---

for the crematory, once all authorizations have been procured. Even then, cremation is not final disposition. After the process, there is still an opportunity for the family to participate in a meaningful and personalized funeral service. The following are two examples.

Services After Cremation

A period of **visitation with the urn** is a service which includes a scheduled time for friends and relatives to visit the family at the funeral home to show support and pay respects to the deceased. Instead of seeing the remains in a casket, however, an urn containing the deceased's cremated remains is present. Placed on a small table or pedestal, the urn may be accompanied by a floral tribute and picture. Other family photos or mementos can also be mounted on a "memory board" or displayed throughout the room. These displays may reflect the deceased's life, occupation, or interests. Some families choose visitation without the urn present, while others prefer private visitation for family members and close friends.

A **memorial service** is generally a service held in a funeral home chapel or place of worship without the remains present. It may be religious or, if the deceased did not profess a specific religious belief, secular. If friends or relatives live in a different part of the country and are unable to travel to one location, more than one memorial service may be held. It is not uncommon to have a memorial service with the urn present. The urn with flowers is displayed on a table or pedestal in front of those in attendance. It is then removed at the end of the service by the funeral director either formally, in the presence of those attending, or informally, after the church has emptied. When a memorial service is held without a period of visitation, some funeral homes provide a guest book at the back of the church or chapel to record the signatures of those in attendance. The book is then given to the family.

Cremation Products

There are literally hundreds of different types of urns and containers available in which to place the cremated remains. Choices between urns must take into account whether the loved one's remains are to be interred, inurned (placed in a niche), or scattered.

There are now a number of manufacturers who offer a full line of personalized urns. This allows families to engrave photos, emblems, and personal information on cast bronze, sheet bronze, hardwood, or marble urns. A number of standard designs can be laser-engraved on the urns, or a custom-design service will engrave black-and-white art on the urn, based on a photo provided by the family. Insignias and emblems representing fraternal interests are also available.

A number of non-traditional companies are emerging with a line of small, decorative vessels and jewelry that are designed to hold a lock of hair or a portion of the cremated remains of a loved one. They are filled and sealed at the funeral home after the completion of the funeral service. The hand-crafted jewelry is available in various shapes and materials including sterling silver, gold-plate, and 14-karat gold with a polished finish. Pendants can be engraved after sealing and come with chains.

Manufacturers have also created a line of keepsake urns, designed as exact miniatures of the larger urns selected to hold the cremated remains. These keepsake urns may be used to hold a portion of the cremated remains or simply serve as a memento. They are crafted in various materials such as cast bronze, hardwood, and marble.

Choosing to Scatter the Remains

When choosing to scatter the remains of your loved one, the selection of the urn is especially important. Those made of bronze, marble, and ceramic can be extremely heavy and somewhat cumbersome to use for scattering. There are, however, urns and containers designed for the easy removal of the cremated remains and are quite suitable for scattering. They are lightweight and usually made of plastic or thin sheet metal. The plastic units are often referred to as "utility" or "temporary" urns, since they are not permanently sealed and may be reopened by popping a lid that snaps into grooved sides. This type of urn is not generally used for display.

Should a family wish a church or chapel service with the urn present prior to scattering, hardwood memento urns have been designed to hold the plastic container. After the service, the memento urn can be used by the family to hold pictures, jewelry, and other personal effects of the deceased, while the plastic urn is discarded after the cremated remains have been scattered. Presentation urns, which can also hold the utility urn, are available for use at a memorial or religious service. These urns need not be purchased but are instead rented from the funeral home. Sheet metal urns are slightly more difficult to open because they are sealed at the bottom with screws. They can, however, be used for display.

A standard urn or container is designed to have a minimum inner volume of approximately 200 cubic inches. This is sufficient to hold the cremated remains of most people. There are, however, occasions when the urn or container selected cannot hold all the cremated remains. In cases like these, the excess is placed in a plastic utility urn, which is also given to the family.

With the exception of urns with narrow openings, the cremated remains are first placed in a plastic liner sealed with a wire tie before placement in the urn. One should always look in the urn or container or discuss how it was filled with a funeral director or crematorium operator before scattering. This will avoid any embarrassment or difficulty one might have when scattering.

For a minimum charge, depending on the location, funeral homes or crematoriums will scatter or arrange for the cremated remains to be scattered for the family.

Permission of the land owner should first be sought if scattering is desired on private property. Permission is not required to scatter cremated remains on public land or in waterways. Some families choose to scatter in such places as a favorite hunting or fishing spot, a country cabin, or at sea.

Cremated remains may also be scattered in cemetery gardens or memorial scattering areas especially created and dedicated for this purpose. The use of dedicated property assures the site chosen will not be developed for other purposes at some future time. Memorial scattering areas range from natural settings to formal gardens. Often, the individuals whose remains have been scattered are identified on a special memorial plaque or inscribed on a unique garden feature such as a sculpture or bench.

Interring Cremated Remains

There are also many options available in cemeteries for the interment or final disposition of cremated remains. These include:

- **Interring the Urn in a Family Plot**—Even when there is no longer room for a casket interment, an existing family plot can accommodate the interment of several urns. Depending on the size and location of existing or proposed monuments, a single grave should be able to accommodate a minimum of three urns.
- **Urn Plots**—For those who prefer traditional earth burial of cremated remains, but do not have or wish to use a family plot, many cemeteries have urn plots set aside. Often these areas are designed around a sculpture or garden feature. Each plot can accommodate the interment of at least one urn.

Columbarium Niches

A popular choice for the placement of an urn is in an indoor or outdoor columbarium niche. A niche is a recessed compartment designed for the permanent placement of urns. A structure housing an arrangement of such niches is called a columbarium. Cemeteries usually offer a wide variety of columbaria from which to choose. Some are free-standing structures located outdoors in picturesque settings. Others are located indoors in either a chapel or mausoleum.

Depending on the location of the niche, it may have an open front protected by glass, where the urn remains visible, or a closed front faced with wood, bronze, granite, or marble, where an inscription is placed. A vase may be installed on some closed-front niches for the placement of flowers by those who care to commemorate special occasions.

As with the mausoleum, sharing the cost of the columbarium with other individuals has made it more affordable.

Memorialization After Scattering

Scattering in remote areas on land or in water prevents a family member from making regular visits to the final resting place and essentially eliminates the opportunity to place a permanent memorial at the site. This may have a negative impact on certain family members. It also conflicts with Christian teaching, which specifies that burial of cremated remains in consecrated ground should be the first option. Most clergy will not insist upon this rule and are often called upon to make compromises. One such compromise is the separation of the cremated remains into two or more containers with one being buried and the contents of the other scattered.

In most places, individuals whose cremated remains are scattered in cemetery or memorial gardens are identified on a plaque or wall, a sculpture, or memorial bench. Even when scattering in remote areas, family members may still choose to erect a permanent marker or place the name of the deceased in a Book of Remembrance. A living memorial, such as a tree suitably identified with a plaque, is another way to remember the deceased.

If the scattering is done at sea, perhaps a point on the coast could become that special place to go. Knowing the latitude and longtitude of the scattering site might also be a comfort. Natural structures, such as a mountain or waterfall located in the area where the scattering occurred could serve as a permanent memorial and a place to go to remember.

Chapter Ten
The Matter of Cost

Twilight and evening bell,
And after that the dark!
And may there be no sadness of farewell,
When I embark
　　　　—Alfred Lord Tennyson, Crossing the Bar

When a loved one dies, family and friends want to pay tribute in the best way possible. Whether that means a traditional funeral service with earth burial or a memorial service with cremation and scattering, survivors deliberate over the smallest details. Often, the selections made are influenced by cost, and funeral directors work within every family's budget to ensure that the final farewell to a loved one is unique, sensitive, and fitting.

Because of the uniqueness of each funeral home and the wide variety of products and services offered, specific costs are difficult to pinpoint. Therefore, this chapter outlines the various components of a traditional or cremation service along with a range of costs for each.

Traditional Funeral Costs

In general, the cost components of a traditional adult funeral service fall into the following four categories: professional services; merchandise costs; out-of-pocket expenses; and cemetery and memorialization costs.

Professional Services

With reference to statistics compiled by the Management Analysis Department of Federated Funeral Directors of America (FFDA) in Springfield, Illinois, a company that serves more than 1,300 client funeral homes in 44 states ranging in size from small rural operations to large volume firms, the average price of a regular adult funeral, which includes a casket and funeral home's professional services is $5,455.00. Depending on the size and location of a funeral home or satellite operation, the professional services component of this figure may vary from $2,600 to over $3,000 with the casket price ranging from $2,400 to $2,800.

The biggest factors affecting this total are the amount of time funeral home staff devote to the arrangements and service, and the fee for the use of funeral home facilities and equipment. Management and staff of a funeral home are on call around the clock and are ready to assist families at any time, on any day. Generally, though, a complete funeral service—from arrangements to follow-up—requires between 60 and 70 person hours.

The costs for staff services include the response to the first call, transportation of the deceased to the funeral home, meeting with family to discuss the funeral service and product selection, gathering vital statistics, and itemizing costs.

Preparation of the deceased, especially for viewing, involves other staff services such as embalming, washing, dressing, applying cosmetics, hairdressing, and reconstructive restoration, when necessary.

In addition, members of the funeral home staff have to coordinate all aspects of the visitation and funeral services. This involves arranging for the services of the priest, rabbi, or spiritual leader, musicians, florists, and transportation between the funeral home, place of worship, and cemetery. It may also include working with other funeral homes, if the preparation of the deceased, funeral service, or burial is taking place elsewhere.

There are also administrative costs, which include completion and procurement of necessary documents such as the death certificate, funeral director's certificate of death, permit for disposition, and clergy record, as well as any forms relating to cremation services. Staff will also inform radio stations and newspapers of the death and order or prepare bulletins for the service at the place of worship, if required.

Included in the facilities and equipment costs are fees to cover the fixed overhead of the funeral home itself along with the use of the facilities during visitation and service. Fixed overhead fees cover such items as taxes, inventory, maintenance, utilities, and insurance. The costs for use of the funeral home facilities include fees for the preparation room, visitation rooms, reception areas, chapel, meeting rooms, kitchen, parking area, and crematorium, if applicable. Transportation fees include use of the funeral coach for the deceased, lead car for clergy, rabbi, or spiritual leader, limousine for family, and a utility vehicle to transport pallbearers, flowers, and equipment to and from the cemetery.

Merchandise Costs

Funeral merchandise includes caskets or containers, burial vaults, urns and a selection of such items as memorial books, prayer cards, crucifixes, or acknowledgment cards. There are a wide variety of caskets and urns available in various sizes, styles, and materials. The cost of each product will depend on many factors, but final price is generally determined by craftsmanship and the types of materials used. Caskets and urns may range in price from a few hundred dollars to several thousand.

The FFDA reports that the average price for an outer burial container is $980. The prices of burial vaults and containers are determined by their design, ease of construction, and the types of materials used. The least expensive unit is the wooden grave liner, which ranges in price between $250 and $350. This is followed by the fiberglass vault, which is priced between $650 and $950. Next is the steel vault, which costs between $950 and $1,250. The concrete vault is considered to be the most expensive. Its costs will depend on certain design features including the number and types of liners, whether an outer casing is used, and how it is personalized. Prices range from under $1,000 for the basic single-walled unit, to several thousand dollars for the triple-walled or the encased bronze or copper units.

Out-of Pocket Expenses

Out-of-pocket expenses are expenses for services not provided directly by the funeral home. Many funeral homes pay these expenses in advance on behalf of the family for their convenience and include them, at cost, on the final invoice.

Examples of these indirect costs are newspaper notices, hairdressing, flowers, organist, soloist, honorarium for clergy, clothing, legal filings, and transportation, if applicable. According to the FFDA, the average out-of-pocket expenses per adult is $745.00.

Cemetery and Memorialization Costs

The costs related to the burial of the deceased include the purchase of a plot and its opening and closing. The fees charged vary, depending on a number of factors including whether the cemetery is owned and operated by a public, private, or religious organization, located in a rural or urban setting, and if it offers perpetual care. Usually cemeteries run by religious organizations in rural settings do not offer perpetual care and, therefore, charge lower fees than the publicly or privately run urban cemeteries that do offer this service. As a result there is a large variance in the cost of a plot and its opening and closing ranging from several hundred to several thousands of dollars. If married, surviving spouses often purchase a double plot. This will increase the average cemetery fee.

Some cemeteries charge an additional fee, which is either a percentage of the cost of the headstone or marker at the time of installation, usually 10 percent, or a flat fee. When married, most couples choose to place a double headstone rather than two singles. Because of the different shapes, sizes, and materials available, upright headstones can cost anywhere from $1,000 for a single stone to over $7,000 for a more elaborate double stone. The cost of a typical double headstone, however, may range from $2,500 to $3,500. The average cost for a bronze marker is $600 for a single and $1,000 for a double.

Cremation Costs

Choosing cremation need not limit funeral service options. On the contrary, it may actually broaden them. The most requested cremation options are as follows:

- Traditional Adult Service followed by cremation—using either a traditional casket, cremation casket, or rental casket with alternative container;
- Direct cremation, visitation, and church/chapel service with urn;
- Direct cremation followed by a memorial service;
- Direct cremation with scattering;
- Direct cremation with graveside committal service and burial of urn—using either a family plot, regular plot, or urn plot.

Traditional Service with Cremation

The cost components of a traditional funeral service ending in cremation are essentially the same as those ending in burial. The professional and staffing services, along with the use of the facilities and equipment, are identical. Any additional costs for cremation services are often offset by the reduction in cemetery costs.

Professional staffing and facilities fees that include the cost of cremation can range from $2,800 to $3,800, depending on the size and location of the funeral home.

When visitation and a church or chapel service are desired, families must also select a casket. Some prefer the design and ornamentation of traditional caskets, which range in price from hundreds to thousands of dollars. Some manufacturers offer cremation caskets, which are less expensive and again range from hundreds to thousands of dollars. Funeral homes may also offer rental caskets to families who choose cremation. These caskets, which have replaceable interiors, can be rented for a few hundred to over a thousand dollars. Rental fees will increase in accordance with casket quality. For example, rental of a solid mahogany casket may exceed $1,500, while a veneer product could be less than $500. Since the deceased must still be cremated in some type of container, certain rental caskets come with a removable wooden or cardboard container inside the rental unit. Families choosing a rental casket without an interior container will have to pay extra for an alternative container. These may range in price from under $100 for a cardboard container to several hundred dollars for a wooden one.

The following demonstrates the difference in cost between cremation services that use these three types of caskets. The figures used are average costs and will vary depending on the quality of the casket or container chosen. They do not include out-of-pocket expenses, cemetery and memorialization costs, or taxes.

Traditional casket
(polished hardwood or equivalent) $2,600
Professional services including cremation $3,300
TOTAL $5,900

Cremation casket (hardwood or equivalent)	$1,800
Professional services including cremation	$3,300
TOTAL	$5,100

Rental casket (hardwood with cremation unit and replaceable interior)	$1,200
Professional services including cremation	$3,300
TOTAL	$4,500

Rental casket (veneer with replaceable interior)	$650
Cremation container (cardboard)	$150
Professional services including cremation	$3,300
TOTAL	$4,100

Direct Cremation, Visitation/Service with Urn

Even though cremation has taken place, some families still choose to have a visitation period and religious or secular service at their place of worship or the funeral home's chapel with the cremated remains present. In this case, the professional and staffing services and use of the facilities and equipment are slightly less than a traditional service and will range from $2,200 to $2,800.

The selection of an urn is a very important component of this type of funeral service, as it provides both a protective and dignified receptacle for the cremated remains. Urns are crafted from various materials such as wood, marble, ceramic, and bronze. Like caskets, urn prices are determined by their design and the types of materials used. Intricately designed bronze urns can cost thousands of dollars, while a plain hardwood urn may cost a few hundred. Most funeral homes display an average of 15 to 25 urns.

Higher-priced urns can range from $1,000 to $2,500, while lower-priced options cost between $150 and $750.

The average cost for this type of service, not including out-of-pocket expenses, memorialization or tax is $2,900—$2,000 for professional services, $275 for crematory fees, $225 for the alternative container, and $400 for a hardwood urn.

Memorial Service

A memorial service is generally held without the cremated remains present. If held in a funeral home chapel, there is usually a charge for the use of this facility. Prices range from $1,000 to $1,400. This includes the costs for the removal of the remains, use of chapel, crematory fees, purchase of an alternative container, administrative, and overhead charges.

Scattering

Charges for direct cremation range from $900 to $1,500. Most families choose to scatter their loved one themselves, either on land or in water, but funeral homes also provide that service for a minimal charge.

Graveside Committal Service

For families wishing to bury their loved one's cremated remains in a cemetery during a public or private committal service, three options are available. The following costs are the average cemetery charges only. Funeral home charges for cremation and attendance at the graveside committal service will add between $1,000 and $1,600 to the final cost.

To inter the deceased's cremated remains in a family plot, it will cost about $1,400, which covers the fee for opening and closing the grave. To inter the deceased in a regular plot, it will cost about $800. To bury the cremated remains in an urn plot, it costs about $1,400, which covers the cost for the plot and fee for the opening and closing.

Chapter Eleven

The Wisdom of Preplanning

In my end is my beginning,
—Mary, Queen of Scots

T he subject of death and final separation from your loved ones are subjects few people are willing to think about, much less discuss. Yet, an increasing number of individuals are choosing to preplan their funerals or those of other family members who may be terminally ill or incapacitated. People choose to preplan to spare their family the responsibility when death occurs or to ensure that their funeral conforms to their wishes. Others might want to make the difficult decisions at a time when they are calm, before grief clouds their or family members' judgment. In addition, preplanners may want to record vital information that might otherwise remain unknown or they may simply want to choose a funeral home in advance.

Regardless of the reason, when a loved one dies after a funeral has been preplanned, family members often tell funeral directors how grateful and relieved they are that the arrangements were made well in advance of the sad day.

The first step to preplanning your funeral or that of a family member who is in poor health is to select the funeral home, cemetery, or memorial society that will serve you and the family. Next, make an appointment with one of their representatives. Meetings can be arranged at their place of business or at one's home, office, or resident care facility, either during the day or in the evening. This meeting allows the funeral planner and family to get to know each other by exchanging information that will greatly assist both parties at the time of need.

To accurately record one's wishes, the funeral planner completes a Preplanning Form. This entails reviewing all aspects of a funeral and/or burial and providing a detailed cost summary of all services and merchandise selected, including third-party expenses. All arrangements are confidential with the original form kept on file at the funeral home, cemetery, or memorial society office and a copy returned to the person making the arrangements.

Prepaying a Funeral

Although not a requirement, the choice to prepay one's funeral and burial service is also available. In addition to relieving survivors of any financial burdens or hardships, one of the main reasons for doing so is to guarantee the cost of the funeral and burial. Once all services identified have been paid in full, the funeral home, cemetery, or memorial society assumes the responsibility for all price increases; this may mean a savings of hundreds or even thousands of dollars for the survivors. Also, before entering a resident care facility, most people choose to put their financial affairs in order. In many cases, this would include the preplanning and prepayment of their funeral and burial expenses.

Prepaying also guarantees the quality of the products you choose. For example, if you chose a casket or urn that is unavailable or is discontinued at the time of death, the funeral home will provide one of similar or higher quality.

In addition to a guaranteed or fixed-price contract, non-guaranteed or non-fixed price contracts are also available. With this type of plan, the funeral is purchased in advance, but the prices are not fixed. At death, the products and services are charged at the current prices. If there is insufficient funds in the account to pay for the original selections, survivors must pay the difference or make alternate choices. Any excess funds are returned to the estate of the deceased. Interest or income earned on both plans must be reported annually on the purchaser's tax return.

A prepaid contract may be canceled at anytime for any reason. If canceled within the recission period, which may be from three to seven days of the contract's execution, all monies are returned. If canceled after the recission period, the funeral home, cemetery, or memorial society may charge an administration fee of not more than 10 or 15 percent of the contract price. If the purchaser is making installment payments, usually no more than half may be applied to a service charge. If the contract is canceled before it is paid in full, unpaid service fees are no longer due. Instead all income or interest earned less a small administrative fee must be returned to the purchaser. In many instances these plans can be transferred to another funeral home, in or out of state.

As the rules and regulations governing prefunded funerals and their cancellation policies may differ from state to state, it is important to review the contract closely and seek clarification, where necessary with the regulatory authority or applicable government department.

Prepayment Options

There are various types of prepayment plans available; however, there are three methods most currently used: the placement of money in trust in federally-insured financial institutions, the purchase of funeral insurance or annuity products, and the establishment of a savings or certificate of deposit account earmarked for funeral expenses and designated as "payable on death" (POD) to the funeral establishment.

Funeral homes, cemeteries, or memorial societies must administer prepaid funeral deposits as per state and federal legislation. Nevertheless, the majority places monies collected into trust accounts, thus protecting them from claims by third parties. Once in the account, the funds are invested in interest-bearing deposits, treasury bills, or other secured investments.

With insurance-funded or annuity plans, an individual may preplan his or her funeral and purchase a funeral insurance policy or annuity, the proceeds of which would be used to pay for the funeral. The funeral home, cemetery, or memorial society would be named the policy or annuity's beneficiary or would receive an assignment of the future death benefit. Insurance or annuity funded plans may be either guaranteed or non-guaranteed contracts depending on whether the policy included a growth component.

With a POD account, the funeral home, cemetery or memorial society will keep a record of an individual's final wishes. The individual then has the option of setting up a savings account or separate trust account at a financial institution of his or her choice to cover the anticipated costs of the funeral and burial services. The plan is not guaranteed and interest or income earned stays in the account. The funeral home, cemetery, or memorial society is named the account's beneficiary with the proceeds payable at the account holder's death.

There are many different types of policies available. Insurance and annuity plans are generally provided by insurance brokers or specifically firms not affiliated with any one particular funeral home, cemetery, or memorial society. Information about some of these plans can be obtained from most of these establishments. In any case, it is important to first identify the cost of the funeral and burial service. Depending on the service provider, the purchaser may be able to refund not only funeral home and cemetery charges, but also any third-party expenses such as flowers, newspaper notices, honoraria, and others.

Funeral Insurance in Detail

Although the marketing of funeral insurance products are strikingly similar, some of them are not as simple and straightforward as they appear and, more important, may not provide the coverage needed when death occurs. From a funeral director's perspective, the following are the key points for consumers to consider when contemplating the purchase of funeral insurance.

Insurance agents are not funeral directors. Although some will have a rudimentary understanding of the average costs of a funeral, with promotional materials to support it, they will have no idea what *your* funeral will cost. Avoid purchasing too little or too much coverage, but make sure you have adequate protection.

Do not purchase any insurance without first preplanning your funeral and identifying the costs of the funeral services and other final expenses. This will give you a clear idea of how much coverage you need.

All persons up to age 85, and in some cases up to age 90, are eligible for funeral insurance. Some companies require no health information whatsoever, while others specify no doctor's examination but will ask you health questions. Funeral insurance is sold on the basis of a person's age, lifestyle, and health. If insurance companies are waiving or minimizing the amount of information required about a person's health or medical condition, there must be a safeguard built into the policies to compensate for the possible poor health of an applicant.

Some insurance companies offer plans that contain a time restriction and limited death benefit before full coverage becomes effective. This is especially true if the applicant does not qualify for full coverage because of health reasons. With these plans, there is usually a time restriction of 18 or 24 months, depending on the term of the policy, when the death benefit will be limited to a return in premiums paid plus an annualized growth rate of three or four percent. But if the insured person dies before this time restriction is up, the insurance may not cover all costs.

Therefore, although one of the important features of this type of insurance is the limited health information required in order to qualify, you should be aware of the restrictions and limitations designed into these policies for those who are in poor health. Make sure that the policy you purchase provides the coverage you need or desire.

For those who do qualify for immediate coverage, who, in this case, are those persons in good health, there are insurance companies that offer whole life insurance products or products with increasing benefits that can be used to prepay prearranged funeral services. In addition, the funeral home will guarantee or hold the cost of the funeral service and other final expenses for the duration of the contract from the date the first premium payment is received by the insurance company.

In such a case, after meeting with a funeral director to preplan your funeral and identify the cost of the funeral services selected, an insurance agent will then meet with you to review the various policies available. Unless additional insurance is required, the coverage selected would coincide with the cost of the funeral services. In order for the costs to be guaranteed by the funeral home, the policy must be assigned by the purchaser to the funeral home. This means that when the death of the purchaser occurs, and the funeral services are rendered, the funeral home will receive the full value of the policy plus the growth component. A special assignment form will be provided by the agent for this purpose.

Failure to keep the assigned policy in force will render it null and void. This will then relieve the funeral home of any further obligation and cause the cancellation of the prefunded funeral services agreement. Therefore, in order to guarantee the cost of your funeral through the use of funeral insurance, ensure that your policy has a growth component, and the funeral home will accept its assignment.

Do not hesitate to investigate or inquire about the insurance company and the products it is offering. Each company should be registered with both state and federal governments. Ask the funeral home if it is aware of the company or has any experience with them.

Determine whether the company provides protection for its policy holders should it experience financial difficulty. According to the Association of Insurance Commissioners (NAIC) all states have established quasi-governmental guarantee associations and require all life insurance companies marketing in the state to join. Therefore, in the event an insurer becomes insolvent, coverage provided by all eligible policies would be continued by the association, generally in accordance with the terms. Consumers would then receive benefits from the association.

Should you wish additional information about NAIC or to confirm whether an insurance company is a member of the state association, visit www.naic.org.

Chapter Twelve
Getting Financial Help

That saints will aid if men will call:
For the blue sky bends over all!
   — Samuel Taylor Coleridge, *Christabel*

W hen faced with the expenses associated with the funeral services of a loved one, many people are unaware of the financial benefits that may be available to eligible survivors to offset some, if not all, of these expenses. Although not an exhaustive list, some of the more common benefits include:

1. **Social Security Benefits**
    If the deceased has worked and paid social security taxes, certain family members may be eligible for survivor benefits, including a lump sum death payment. Up to ten years of work is needed to be eligible for benefits, depending on the deceased's age at the time of death. Beneficiaries may include the spouse, dependent children, and dependent parents of the deceased.

    When the surviving spouse is living with the deceased at the time of death or, if living apart, is eligible for Social Security benefits based on the deceased's earnings record for the month of death, he or she will receive a one-time lump sum death benefit of $255. When there is no surviving spouse, the payment is made to a dependent child.

In order to apply for Social Security benefits a family member or other person responsible for the deceased's affairs should promptly notify the Social Security Office by calling their nationwide toll-free number 1-800-772-1213.

For more information about filing benefits, in addition to calling the toll-free number, you may visit their website at www.ssa.gov.

2. **Social Assistance**
For those individuals who die without an estate or financial resources, the cost of funeral and burial services are generally taken care of by the municipality or county through their department of social services. Although the funding provided by each municipality or county may differ, the funeral services provided, usually include the funeral director's professional services and use of facility and equipment, legal filings, transportation of the remains, the provision of a cloth-covered casket, clothing, grave with opening and closing or cremation services, a funeral notice, and clergy

honorarium. Some jurisdictions will also include an annual cost of living increase for the funeral director and other service providers.

3. **Veteran Benefits**
   The U.S. Department of Veteran Affairs (VA) offers a wide range of benefits and services to honor the nation's deceased veterans. Generally, they will pay a burial allowance of $2,000 for veterans who die of service-related causes. For other veterans, they will pay $300 for burial and funeral expenses and $300 for a plot. Veteran's Affaires will also furnish a monument to mark the grave of an eligible veteran.

   The burial benefits available for veterans wishing to be interred in any of the 120 national cemeteries with available space include a gravesite, opening and closing of the grave, perpetual care, a government headstone or marker, a burial flag and a Presidential Memorial Certificate, at no cost to the family.

   There is no time restriction for claiming reimbursement of burial expenses for a service-related death.In other cases, claims must be filed within two years of the veteran's burial. For more information about VA burial and memorial benefits visit www.va.gov.

4. **Active Service Member Benefits**
   The Armed Forces will pay all funeral costs and benefits for active war deaths, includ-

ing an insurance policy that ranges from $125,000 to $250,000. A cheque for $6,000 is issued almost immediately to the next-of-kin to assist with initial expenses. Children also receive education benefits and a monthly check, as does the spouse.

5. **Worker's Compensation**
   If death occurs as a result of an accident or other circumstances occurring in the workplace, the Worker's Compensation Commission of each state, with the exception of New Mexico, Rhode Island, and Louisiana, will pay a death benefit towards funeral expenses to, or on behalf of, the estate of the deseased. The maximum benefits available vary from state to state, ranging from $2,000 to $10,000 with one state, Kentucky, paying all expenses. Some states also provide additional funds for transportation and provision of a headstone. Members of volunteer fire companies, emergency medical, and rescue services may also receive an additional funeral benefit of not less than $100 and as high as $1,500 in some states.

6. **Crime Victims Compensation**
   To provide financial assistance to crime victims who have died as a result of criminal activities some states have established crime victims' compensation programs. In certain jurisdictions, a death benefit of up to a

maximum of $2,500 for funeral expenses may be paid.

7. **Company and Union Benefits**
   If the deceased was working, there may be benefits available from the union or the employer.

8. **Life Insurance**
   One of the most common survivor benefits is life insurance. The funeral director, if requested, will assist with the completion of claim forms and the provision of any information or documentation. Depending on the insurance company, a Funeral Director's Statement of Death may be the only document necessary in order for a claim to be processed. Otherwise, a certified copy of the death certificate, available from the Registrar of the District in which the death occurred or the State Registrar.

9. **Fraternal Organizations**
   Some fraternal organizations provide death benefits to the families of their members. As many of these benefits go unclaimed because families are not aware of their existence, it would be prudent to advise the funeral director of clubs, lodges, or associations to which the deceased belonged.

10. **Bereavement Airfares**
    Bereavement or compassionate travel airfares are available for both domestic and in-

ternational travel. They are not always the least expensive seats as only certain classes of seats are market for bereavement discount. Check for the lowest available fares before asking if there are bereavement seats available.

Chapter Thirteen

The Funeral Home
& Its Professionals

Blessed are they that mourn;
for they shall be comforted
— Matthew 5:4

The death of a loved one is one of the most difficult, emotionally challenging events in anyone's life. In addition to family members and
friends, the help from funeral home staff is integral to
the resolution of your grief. But most people know
very little about the men and women who dedicate
their careers to helping others in the most trying of
times. They know even less about the funeral profession itself and its training and regulatory controls. The
following describes the funeral home, the professionals who work in it, and emerging trends in funeral
service.

The Funeral Home

In recent years, funeral service has experienced significant change, but none as profound as the changes occurring to the funeral home itself. Existing facilities are
being remodelled and new facilities constructed using

unique designs and layouts. Consumers' expectations are changing, too. Recognizing this, funeral home owners and operators are expanding the services and products they provide by enhancing their facilities.

This has led to an unprecedented growth in new funeral home construction and the remodelling and expansion of existing funeral homes. Large, modern facilities are being designed and built to provide the public with a more spacious, home-like environment. Well-appointed lobbies, reposing rooms, and lounges are being enlarged or added for the comfort and convenience of families and friends. Additional services are also being provided with the installation of crematoriums, chapels, and reception centers.

In order to meet the trend of providing a greater product choice for consumers, leading funeral homes are developing professional merchandising plans. This has required the complete remodelling of casket selection rooms, the addition of cremation and other funeral-related products, and vast improvements in organizing, classifying, and displaying these products.

Funeral Home Design

The centerpiece of any funeral home is its front entrance and lobby. To protect the public from inclement weather and to accentuate its entrance, many facilities have roof overhangs or porticos for vehicles. These structures are often supported by large columns, which also add to their elegance. The funeral home lobby has now become the focal point of the building, connecting all other public areas such as the business and arrangement offices, reposing rooms, lounges, and chapel. Its decor and design are usually very similar to a residence or hotel lobby and feature high ceilings, chandeliers, fireplaces, and elaborate furnishings.

Architects are also using large decorative windows in entrance ways to introduce more natural light into the space. This is an element which is sadly lacking in many older funeral homes. Marble flooring and stained glass windows have also been used very effectively in lobby designs.

There have been many changes made to the arrangement office, as well. In the past, family members sat in front of the funeral director, who was at a desk recording pertinent information. Today, the family and funeral director take their seats around a table and complete the arrangements in surroundings considered to be more intimate and personal. Other features added to the office include attractive paintings and plants, soft lighting, cabinets, and bookshelves. If the arrangement office is next to the casket selection room, some funeral directors also display a variety of urns. When not in use for arrangements, some use the area as a resource center where books, videos, and other materials about death, dying, and bereavement are available to the public.

Like cremation, the use of funeral home chapels is a growing trend in the industry. More and more funeral homes and cemeteries are adding chapels to accommodate transient families, those no longer affiliated with a church, small families who are reluctant to use large churches, and churches themselves who can no longer afford the high costs of heat and electricity.

The most recent addition to a funeral home facility has been the reception center, an area dedicated solely to the gathering of family, relatives, and friends after the funeral and committal service. It is in addition to the lounge or lounges used by the family during the visitation period. Also referred to as a "community room" or "coffee lounge," this area includes a small kitchen and spacious lounge with tables and chairs. Instead of going to someone's home, family and friends return to the reception center where the funeral home arranges catering services.

Vast improvements have been made in the manner in which caskets, urns, and other funeral-related products are organized, classified, and displayed. Traditionally, caskets were displayed on biers or pedestals in no particular order and in a poorly lit, sparsely decorated room. In today's modern selection room, the design, decor, and lighting combine to enhance the quality of the merchandise and the appearance of the room. The same design principles are used for cremation-related products, ideally in a separate selection room. This provides sufficient space to display a wide variety of cremation caskets and urns of different materials, styles, and prices.

Training for Funeral Service

How does one become a licensed funeral director and embalmer? Students wishing to pursue a career in funeral service must first complete an accredited funeral service education program. All issues and decisions regarding accreditation of programs are the sole responsibility of the American Board of Funeral Service Education's Committee of Accreditation (COA). For more information call 207-878-6530.

The COA is an autonomous committee within the American Board. It is recognized by the U.S. Department of Education and the Council of Higher Education Accreditation as the only accrediting body for funeral service education in the United States.

The total number of accredited programs is 52, located in 30 states and the District of Columbia. New York has the largest number of accredited programs with five; Illinois, Mississippi, and Texas are close behind with four. The 20 states without programs are generally across the northern tier of states from Washington in the west to Maine in the east.

Programs are also available online and by television instruction. None of the accredited programs offer the entire funeral service degree at a distance because student are required to complete supervised embalming and restorative art classes on campus.

Women in Funeral Service

For years, a career in funeral service was considered men's work. Many funeral home owners and managers would not consider hiring a female funeral director because they believed women were not physically or emotionally capable of handling the rigors of funeral service. Today, a female funeral director/embalmer is an asset a funeral home owner or manger can ill afford to overlook.

According to the American Board of Funeral Service Education (ABFSE) the number of women enrolling in funeral service education continues its past growth and in 2000, for the first time in history, the number of female first-time students was greater than the number of males.

Male/Female Enrollment

Year	Male	Female	%Female
1971	1762	103	5%
1976	2210	343	13%
1981	1753	417	19%
1986	1577	538	25%
1991	1873	785	34%
1996	1936	1277	40%
1999	1481	1309	47%
2000	1169	1199	51%
2001	1109	1141	51%
2002	1255	1290	51%

Source: American Board of Funeral Service Education

Of the total number of students enrolled, just over 80 percent have passed their National Board Exam since 2000. Concern has been expressed by various industry groups that the number of graduates is not going to meet the workforce needs of the funeral service industry in the next few years. A task force on Workforce Issues and Enrollment has been struck to address this issue.

Women's emotions, mannerisms, and expressions are different than men's and have their own appeal. Having a female funeral director/embalmer on staff provides a real balance within a funeral home setting and is generally appreciated by the family members, relatives, and friends of the deceased.

Licensing

For most students, the challenge begins after graduation with finding a job and then obtaining a license. Before a student is eligible to receive a license, he or she must undergo a 12-month internship or apprenticeship training program in a licensed funeral home under the direction of a licensed funeral director/embalmer.

As most states do not have a formal internship training program, obtaining a quality internship that will enhance and augment a student's formal education can also be a challenge. For those states that do, interns are required to complete a certain number of preparations and conduct a certain number of arrangement conferences. Again, these requirements vary from state to state. Those funeral homes who understand the value of on-the-job training and professional staff development may require an intern to spend six month in the preparation room and the remaining six months with an arranger.

At the end of the 12-month apprenticeship program, interns must then pass licensing exams. State Board licensing examinations vary, but usually they consist of written and oral parts and include a demonstration of practical skills. Upon the successful completion of these exams, the interns receive their credentials as licensed funeral directors and embalmers. Licensing regulations also vary from state to state. For example, in some states only one license is required for both disciplines, while others require one license for a funeral director and another license for an embalmer.

Reciprocal Licensing

Licensed funeral directors and embalmers wishing to work in a state other than the one in which they received their license, may have to pass the licensing examinations for that state. Some states, however, have reciprocal licensing arrangements and will grant licenses to funeral directors and embalmers from another state without further examination. These arrangements effectively eliminate residency, curriculum, and other barriers impeding or preventing licensed funeral professionals from seeking employment in a state other than their place of residence.

Regulation of the Funeral Profession

The regulatory control of licensed funeral professionals comes under the jurisdiction of the state. Most states have a licensing board appointed by the state with members from the funeral profession, the public at large and government. The Federal Trade Commission of the U.S. government enforces the Funeral Rule. It is the Funeral Rule that governs the conduct of funeral homes or the overall funeral industry. It cannot deal with individual complaints but can take action against funeral homes for any infringements of the Rule.

The Licensing Board's primary function is to regulate licensing of funeral directors, embalmers, and funeral homes and the coordination of funeral service education and continuing education programs. The Board also addresses any violation of state legislation that governs the industry.

The Board has the authority to define what constitutes incompetence and misconduct of embalmers and funeral directors. It has established procedures to deal with complaints from fellow practitioners. But, more importantly, the Board has an obligation to the public. It is also part of the mandate to hear and, if deemed warranted, take action concerning complaints from consumers or family members. These complaints may be associated with the practices or conduct of either a funeral home or its licensed staff.

If you have a problem concerning funeral matters, it is best to try to resolve it first with the funeral director. If that should prove unsuccessful, consumers may contact the State Licensing Board for information or help.

Consumers can also file a complaint with the Funeral Trade Commission by contacting the Consumer Response Center by phone, toll free, at 1-877-FTC-HELP (382-4357) or visit their Web site at www.ftc.gov and use the online complaint form.

These are not the only avenues available to the general public should they have concerns or complaints respecting funeral service. Consumers may also register complaints with the appropriate government department, such as those with jurisdiction over legal matters or consumer and corporate affairs.

Appendix

Funeral Checklist

❑ Choose a funeral home

❑ What type of service is desired (traditional or cremation)

❑ Record personal information

❑ Wording for funeral notice

❑ Select clothing

❑ A list of people who should be notified

❑ Select casket, urn, or burial vault or liner

❑ If traditional service, will casket be opened or closed

❑ Select celebrant and location of funeral service

❑ Confirm people or organizations who should assume key roles (i.e., pallbearers, speakers, veterans, fraternal)

❑ Consider ways to personalize the service (i.e., favorite hymn(s), music, readings, memorabilia)

❑ Create rituals that would have special meaning to family and friends

❑ If cremation service, what will happen to the cremated remains

❑ If burial, select cemetery

❑ Floral tribute (casket spray, cross, or special arrangement)

Afterword

Geoffrey C. Carnell Jr. is the President of Carnell's Funeral Home in St. John's, Newfoundland, Canada. A professional Engineer and licensed Funeral Director, Carnell heads a business that has passed through six generations of his family.

Established in 1804, the Carnell Carriage Factory originally manufactured horse-drawn carriages and sleighs. As carpenters, the Carnells were often approached by members of the community to build wooden containers in which to bury deceased family members or friends. They would deliver these "containers or coffins" to the location of the wake. It wasn't long before they were asked to also take charge of funeral and burial services. In the early 1900s, Andrew Carnell became directly involved in undertaking and embalming, graduating from the United States School of Embalming in Chicago. He was the first certified embalmer in Newfoundland.

His son, Geoffrey C. Carnell Senior, became President and Managing Director in 1934 when Andrew Carnell retired from the business to enter local politics. This was the year the company became incorporated. In 1974, Geoffrey Carnell Sr. changed the name of the company to

Carnell's Limited; it operated five divisions, including a funeral home, spring shop, muffler shop, a sales agency, and office/warehouse rental.

The company passed to the author, Geoffrey C. Carnell Junior, on the death of Carnell Sr. in 1987. Carnell Jr. was, at the time, a professional engineer with a municipal consulting firm. He is now also a licensed Funeral Director, as well as President and Managing Director of the company.

Carnell Jr. has instituted many changes to his business premises. In 1988 he introduced a crematorium and a commital area, as well as new offices in 1991. In the mid-1990s he enlarged and enhanced the reposing rooms and lounges, added a foyer, and extended the chapel. He has kept abreast of new developments in the funeral industry, both in technology and in customer relations and requirements. He writes articles on these subjects for *50Plus* magazine, a periodical for seniors. His commitment to providing useful information and services to his clients, his community, and his industry influenced the creation of this book.